Top 25 locator map
(continues on inside
back cover)

◄

CityPack
Prague *Top 25*

MICHAEL IVORY

If you have any comments
or suggestions for this guide
you can contact the editor at
Citypack@theAA.com

AA Publishing
Find out more about AA Publishing and the
wide range of services the AA provides by
visiting our website at *www.theAA.com*

About This Book

KEY TO SYMBOLS

 Map reference to the accompanying fold-out map and Top 25 locator map

⊠ Address

☎ Telephone number

🕐 Opening/closing times

🍴 Restaurant or café on premises or nearby

🚉 Nearest railway station

Ⓜ Nearest Metro station

🚌 Nearest bus route

🚢 Nearest riverboat or ferry stop

♿ Facilities for visitors with disabilities

✋ Admission charges: Expensive (over Kč200), Moderate (Kč50–Kč200), and Inexpensive (Kč50 or less)

⬌ Other nearby places of interest

❓ Other practical information

▶ Indicates the page where you will find a fuller description

ℹ Tourist information

ORGANIZATION

This guide is divided into six chapters:
- Planning Ahead, Getting There
- Living Prague—Prague Now, Prague Then, Time to Shop, Out and About, Walks, Prague by Night
- Prague's Top 25 Sights
- Prague's Best—best of the rest
- Where To—detailed listings of restaurants, hotels, shops and nightlife
- Travel Facts—practical information

In addition, easy-to-read side panels provide extra facts and snippets, highlights of places to visit and invaluable practical advice.

The colours of the tabs on the page corners match the colours of the triangles aligned with the chapter names on the contents page opposite.

MAPS

The fold-out map in the wallet at the back of this book is a comprehensive street plan of Prague. The first (or only) grid reference given for each attraction refers to this map. **The Top 25 locator map** found on the inside front and back covers of the book itself is for quick reference. It shows the Top 25 Sights, described on pages 26–50, which are clearly plotted by number (**1**–**25**, not page number) across the city. The second map reference given for the Top 25 Sights refers to this map.

Contents

Planning Ahead

WHEN TO GO

The best times to visit are in spring, when the fruit trees of Petřín Hill are in blossom, and in early summer, before the throngs of tourists arrive. Most tourists visit between May and September. Christmas and New Year are also busy, with the main squares converted into decorated markets and later into rowdy New Year's Eve party sites.

TIME

Prague is one hour ahead of the UK, six hours ahead of New York and nine hours ahead of Los Angeles.

AVERAGE DAILY MAXIMUM TEMPERATURES

JAN	FEB	MAR	APR	MAY	JUN	JUL	AUG	SEP	OCT	NOV	DEC
30°F	32°F	39°F	48°F	57°F	63°F	66°F	64°F	57°F	48°F	39°F	32°F
-1°C	0°C	4°C	9°C	14°C	17°C	19°C	18°C	14°C	9°C	4°C	0°C

Spring (March–May) starts out cold and damp but turns beautiful in April and May, with blooming trees and gardens throughout the city.
Summer (June–August) can be oppressively hot and humid , with considerable rainfall.
Autumn (September–November) is a lovely time , with bright, sunny days through October and dwindling numbers of tourists. The weather cools considerably by November.
Winter (December–February) can be depressingly grey and cold, with high levels of air pollution.

WHAT'S ON

April/May *Agharta Prague Jazz Festival*: Going strong since 1992, this festival brings in well-known jazz and blues acts from all over. Sponsored by the Agharta jazz club and held in venues throughout the city.
May *Prague Spring Music Festival* (mid-May): This international event consists of an array of classical music concerts in churches, palaces and halls. It starts with a procession from Smetana's grave in the National Cemetery in Vyšehrad to the great hall

named after him in the re-stored Obecní dům (Municipal House), where a rousing performance of his orchestral tone poem *Má Vlast* (My Country) is given.
June *Dance Prague*: Dance festival with events at various venues, including outdoor spaces.
July/August *Open Air Opera Festival*: The Lichtenstejnský palác (Liechtenstein Palace) hosts one of the many musical events held in historic buildings and gardens across the city.

December *St. Nicholas* (5 December): A multitude of St. Nicks roam the streets, accompanied by an angel who rewards good children with candy and a devil who chastizes appropriately.
Christmas Eve (24 December): Live carp are sold on the streets for the traditional Czech Christmas Eve dinner.
New Year's Eve (31 December): There are for-mal Sylvester balls and, outside, crowds welcome the arrival of the New Year on the streets.

Prague Online

www.pis.cz
Information on museums, cultural programmes and Prague history, along with tips, accommodation and general tourist information from the Prague Information Service.

www.praguepost.com
Local news plus restaurant and entertainment listings from one of Prague's English-language newspapers.

www.czechtourism.cz
The Czech Tourist Authority's website provides information on agrotourism, UNESCO-graded monuments, cycling, mountaineering and other outdoor activities, along with practical planning information.

www.prague-tourist-information.com
Includes comprehensive advice on transport, tourist tips, sightseeing, museums, a restaurant guide and a section on children's Prague.

www.radio.cz
News, history, interesting features and information on upcoming events from Radio Prague.

www.czech.cz
The Foreign Ministry's site has specifics on travelling, studying and doing business in the Czech Republic.

www.prague2001.com
Plenty of useful tips for your trip to Prague plus good coverage on nightlife.

www.muselik.com
Czech history, travelogues, recipes, travel tips, plus lots of links from the Czech Information Centre.

www.xs4-all.nl/~patto1ro/pragintr.htm
The Prague Pub Guide features tips and a helpful insight into beer-drinking and pub-going in Prague.

USEFUL TRAVEL SITE

www.fodors.com
A complete travel-planning site. You can research prices and weather; book air tickets, cars and rooms; pose questions to fellow travellers; and find links to other sites.

CYBERCAFÉS

Café Net
A utilitarian café/bar serving hot and cold drinks.
➕ E4 ✉ Havelská (in the passage), Staré Město ☎ 224 213 265 ⏰ 10–10 🎫 20 kč/15 minutes Ⓜ Můstek

The Globe
Coffee, food, books, newspapers and the Internet–the Globe has it all. Plug-ins for laptops.
➕ E5 ✉ Pštrossova 6, Nové Město ⏰ 224 934 203 🎫 1.3 kč/per minute Ⓜ Nádrodní třída

Kav Kava Kava
Voted 'best coffee' in Prague. Café upstairs; computers downstairs.
➕ D–E5 ✉ Národní 37 (in the Platýz courtyard), Staré Město ☎ 224 228 862 ⏰ 1.5–2 kč/per minute Ⓜ Nádrodní třída

Getting There

ENTRY REQUIREMENTS

Tourists from the UK, US and most European countries do not need visas; Canadian visitors do. Check latest requirements before travelling.

MONEY

The Czech crown (*koruna česká* or Kč) is divided into 100 virtually worthless hellers (*haléř*). There are coins for 50 hellers, and for 1, 2, 5, 10, 20 and 50 crowns, and notes in denominations of 20, 50, 100, 200, 500, 1,000, 2,000 and 5,000 crowns.

20 Korun

50 Korun

100 Korun

200 Korun

ARRIVING

Ruzyně Airport is 17km (10 miles) west of Prague city centre and is served by direct flights from most major European cities, as well as New York and Montréal. There are shops, bars and a cafeteria. The national airline is ČSA (head office: ✉ V Celnící 5, Nové Mesto ☎ 2010 4111).

2km (15 miles)   16km (10 miles)   9km (5 miles)   Prague

ARRIVING BY AIR

Airport information ☎ 220 113 321; www.csa.cz
The best link from Ruzyně Airport to the city centre is by shuttle bus to Náměstí Republiky, on the eastern edge of the Old Town. The bus runs from 5.30am–9.30am every half hour. Pick up the white minibus at the Dedaz sign in front of the terminal. The trip takes 20–30 minutes and costs 90kč each way, bags included. Buy your ticket from the driver.

City bus 119 goes to Dejvická station. Pick it up across the carpark in front of the airport. Buy a 12kč ticket inside at the newspaper stand first. The trip takes about 20 minutes and the buses run from 5am until midnight.

Taxis can be picked up at the airport, but you'll pay much less if you call ahead. Agree on the approximate fare before you travel. The cost is around 350–400kč and the journey takes 20–30 minutes.

ARRIVING BY TRAIN

Express trains connect Prague to all neighbouring countries, as well as to Paris, from where passengers can take the EuroStar Channel Tunnel rail link to London. Most trains terminate at Hlavní nádraží (Main Station ✚F4), though some stop (or terminate) at Holešovice in the northern suburbs or at Smíchov in the southern suburbs, both of which have good Metro connections. Czech Railways (ČD) has information offices in Main Station at the north end of level 3 (domestic) and the south end of the lower hall (international) ☎ 224 224 200; www.idos.datis. cdrail.cz

ARRIVING BY CAR

Good main roads link Prague to all neighbouring countries, and the motorway to Plzeň (Pilsen) and the border with Bavaria is almost complete. Prague is 1,100km (683 miles) from Calais (France), with its ferry services to Dover (UK) as well as the Channel Tunnel Shuttle. For more information on driving in the Czech Republic ► panel.

ARRIVING BY BUS

Express buses link Prague with international destinations, including London. The main coach terminal is at Florenc, on the eastern edge of the city centre, where there is also a Metro station. You can buy tickets at the coach terminal in Florenc but it is easier to use a travel agency.

GETTING AROUND

Prague's transport system is based on the immaculate Metro and the less pristine but equally reliable trams and buses. Daily services run from 5am until midnight, when infrequent night buses and trams take over. Inexpensive tickets obtained at stations, kiosks and some hotels serve all three modes and must be validated by inserting into the clipping machine as you enter a station or board a vehicle. Normal tickets are valid for 60 minutes on work days and 90 minutes at weekends, holidays and at night, and allow unlimited transfers among modes; non-transferable tickets are useful for brief trips.
Prague taxi drivers have a reputation for overcharging and being disagreeable.
For more information on getting around ► 91.

INSURANCE

All visitors should have full travel insurance. UK citizens may enjoy free medical treatment in an emergency, but taking out medical insurance ensures rapid repatriation and can help in cutting through bureaucracy.

DRIVING

To drive on Czech motorways you need a toll sticker, which can be bought at the border or at post offices or fuel stations (Kč100 for 10 days; Kč200 for one month). Check that your insurance policy covers you to drive in the Czech Republic. The drink-drive limit is zero alcohol. No special licence is needed for tourists who stay less than 90 days.

VISITORS WITH DISABILITIES

Many of the things that make Prague an enchanting city—cobblestoned streets Gothic towers with breathtaking views and red trams—can be notoriously difficult for visitors with disabilities to negotiate. The Metro, too, has limited access; check which stations have facilities first.

Living
Prague

Prague Now

Above: *A crowd of people on Prague's Old Town Square (Staromestske nam)*
Above right: *Charles Bridge*
Opposite left: *The ground floor café of Prague's art nouveau Evropa Hotel on Wenceslas Square*

Prague is changing fast. With the Czech Republic joining the European Union in 2004, people are looking to the future, and the country can no longer be thought of merely as 'post-communist'. Yet the city is defined as much by the past as by the present. Situated squarely in *Mitteleuropa*, between East and West, it is also trapped, in a sense, between the past and the future.

That is only one of Prague's many paradoxes. This is where the Slavic world meets the Germanic, where Catholic festivity meets Protestant simplicity, where the mystic meets the bureaucratic and the surreal the mundane.

NEIGHBOURHOODS

• An idea of the histories and personalities of Prague's neighbourhoods can sometimes be gleaned from their names. Vinohrady, for instance, means 'vineyards', and this leafy neighbourhood was indeed formerly home to the royal vineyards. Podolí, down by the Vltava river, means 'along the valley'. The tough, working-class district of Žižkov, whose hill was the site of a great Hussite victory, is named for General Jan Žižka, whose equestrian statue is one of the city's dominant features. Dejvice literally means 'give more', though 'own more' might seem a more appropriate name for this well-to-do area. Smíchov was apparently once the home to great laughers (*smích* means laughter).

Czechs are reclaiming Prague after a decade of 'Wild West capitalism', during which Westerners arrived in droves, ready to make a buck. Now it is the Czechs who are opening the sleek, modern hotels, daring fusion restaurants and unique fashion boutiques, showing again the sense for design shown between the wars. At that time—as Germany to the west was staggering under economic collapse and the rising tide of National Socialism and the Soviet Union to the east was the scene of brutal repression and Stalinist show trials—Czechoslovakia was among the world's most industrialized and democratic countries. Prague was a crucible of avant-garde art, theatre and music. Today, after some 40 years of forget-fulness and a decade of difficult transition, Prague is reawakening to the possibilities that were stunted by occupation, war and totalitarianism.

A new generation is finding its footing. Multilingual, well-educated and possessing the trademark Czech dose of cynicism, young people who barely remember communism are not afraid to take risks. Before World War II, Czechs were known for their entrepreneurial spirit and busi-ness acumen, and those traits are again visible.

Above left: Cobbled streets and traditional architecture are part of Prague's charm
Above: Art student on Charles Bridge, sketching the surrounding buildings

GET LOST

● Prague is a labyrinth, a warren of winding roads and alleyways, courtyards and passageways leading deep into buildings. Don't worry about getting lost—treat disorientation as a pleasure and enjoy the unexpected treats along the way. The historic centre is small and sooner or later you will recognize a landmark or emerge by the riverside.

11

Below: *Prague's tree-lined Wenceslas Square in the early evening*

Above right: *The astronomical clock (Orloj) on Town Hall in Old Town Square (Staromestska namesti)*

QUIET PLEASE

• Czechs are not prone to public displays of emotion, bursts of temper or spontaneous singing. On public transport they converse in low voices, if at all; loudly chattering foreigners turn heads and attract pickpockets. Though conversation is animated in pubs and cafés, voices are rarely raised, and shouting is definitely reserved for emergencies and loud work sites.

Walk down any street and you'll see the evidence—tastefully apportioned cafés, well-run art galleries, gorgeous bouquets spilling out of innumerable flower shops.

To be sure, for a few years after the fall of communism, it seemed that picturesque Prague might be buried under an avalanche of crystal trinkets, Russian fur hats and other kitschy tourist dross. Unsuspecting tourists drank overpriced coffee—and worse yet, overpriced beer—at featureless cafés and restaurants that mushroomed along the tourist track. It was becoming difficult, sometimes, to see the charms of the city itself.

Thankfully, the forces are balancing out. People want to see the real Prague, not a made-for-tourists version, and Czechs are relearning how to make the most of their gorgeous city. Unique little shops selling everything from handmade paper to handblocked linens are popping up, and restaurants all over the city are doing a booming business. Neighbourhoods outside the tourist areas are slowly but surely brightening up and offering more variety in food, entertainment and shopping.

Left: *Wenceslas Square*
Above: *Tyn Church*

The Czechs are known for industriousness and resourcefulness and found these qualities much in demand in August 2002. The catastrophic flood temporarily shut down Prague and wrought tremendous damage throughout the country, threatening livelihoods built up with such hard work over the past decade and damaging historic monuments only recently restored.

MONUMENTALLY STRANGE

Prague is home to a number of whimsical works of art:

• An upside-down version of the statue of St. Wenceslas hangs from the ceiling of the Lucerna passage on Wenceslas Square. The horse's lolling tongue is best appreciated at eye level from an upstairs café.
• The Žižkov TV tower has been adorned by sculptor David Černý, with a gang of giant babies that cling to the structure like ants.
• The plinth where Stalin's statue once stood holds a huge metronome, the significance of which no one seems able to explain. In the days leading up to the EU referendum in June 2003, large signs reading 'yes' and 'no' were added to either side of the swinging arm.

TACKLING URBAN DECAY

• Visitors are sometimes shocked at the shabby state of some of Prague's buildings. Under Communism, showpieces were restored at great public expense, but less favoured buildings mouldered away, encased in straitjackets of scaffolding to stop them falling into the street. Privatization and restitution, the return of property to its former owners, has gone far to remedy the situation.

13

Above: *Prague's Old Town*
Above right: *The statues of the Virgin with St Dominic and St Thomas Aquinas on the second pier of Charles Bridge*

The extent of the damage was almost too much to grasp at first. Houses on the picturesque Kampa Island were flooded halfway up their second storeys. In the residential Karlín area, whole apartment buildings collapsed and Metro stations were filled with water. And though the streets of the Old Town remained dry, the water came up from below, forcing its way into the web of centuries-old cellars, almost to street level, until the Old Town was quite literally floating.

But as soon as the raging waters receded, people got down to work. The clean-up operation seemed to give people an excuse to clear out decades—or perhaps centuries—worth of useless rubbish from their cellars. Restaurants and shops gamely renovated and threw open their doors again. The city's efficient system of replacement

USEFUL CZECH PHRASES

- *To je hronzné*. 'That's awful', best muttered on an overcrowded tram or when commenting on graffiti.
- *Ježišmarija*. This means just what it sounds like but it is not considered in the least bit offensive. Routinely uttered by everyone from age four and up.

trams and buses ran until, one by one, the Metro stations reopened. Today the evidence of the flood has been reduced to lines and the date marked on walls to show incredulous visitors how high the river really was.

Most people now have heard about the beauties of Prague—the stunning architecture that spans a millennium, the rich cultural offerings, the cozy pubs serving the world's best beer. But what makes the city great?

In the end, only a handful of cities in the world seem to be more than just bricks and mortar, streets and squares. These few cities—and Prague is certainly one of them—seem to breath, to watch, to live a life of their own. Like Prague, these cities have a soul—and sometimes, it can seem, a will of their own. Kafka wrote about Prague: 'This little mother has claws'. The city pulls you in, wraps you in her embrace and then refuses to let you go'. Even those here for a short time are likely to meet at least one person who says he came to Prague for a few days...several years ago. Most find it hard to leave. Let Prague embrace you, too.

Glasses filled with some of the strong local beer

VITAL STATISTICS

- Prague has a population of 1.2 million.

- Czechs drink an average of 160 litres of beer per person per year.

- Prague's industries, heating plants and motor vehicles emit more than 30,000 tonnes of sulphur dioxide per year.

- The city's historic core includes 10,000 protected artefacts and works of art.

15

Prague Then

Left to right: *White crosses in the paving stones the Old Town Hall chapel mark where Protestant leaders, Czechs and Germans were executed as rebels in June 1621; Jewish Quarter; Prague Castle and buildings of the Hradcany; Václav Klaus*

WHITE MOUNTAIN

In 1620 the Protestant army was routed at the Battle of White Mountain. In the following years, Protestant leaders were executed in Old Town Square. Czechs who refused to reconvert to Catholicism emigrated en masse. A largely foreign nobility was installed, loyal to the Habsburgs, and Prague was beautified with Baroque churches and palaces. The court made Vienna its principal seat and Prague became a sleepy provincial town.

7th or 8th century AD	Prague's legendary foundation by Princess Libuše and her ploughman husband, Přemysl.
10th century	Trading settlements are set up in Lesser Town and Old Town.
1231	King Wenceslas I fortifies the Old Town with 13 towers, 12m-high walls and a moat (today's Na Příkopě, or Moat Street).
1253–78	Reign of King Otakar II, who extends and fortifies Lesser Town, inviting German merchants to settle there.
1576–1611	Reign of eccentric Emperor Rudolph II.
1620	Battle of White Mountain (➤ panel).
1848	Austrian General Windischgrätz puts down a revolt led by students, but Czech nationalism continues to grow.
1914–18	Czechs are dragged against their will into World War I on the Austrian side. Many soldiers desert or join the Czechoslovak Legion fighting for the Allies.
1918	The democratic First Republic of Czechoslovakia is established under liberal president Tomáš Garrigue Masaryk.

1939 Prague is declared the 'Fourth City of the Third Reich' (► side panel).

1945 The people of Prague liberate their city and welcome in the Red Army.

1948 Communists, the most powerful party in the democratically elected goverment, stage a coup d'état. Stalinist repression follows.

1968 Prague Spring (► side panel).

1977 Dissident intellectuals sign Charter 77, a call for the government to apply the Helsinki Agreements of 1975. Many harrassed and imprisoned.

1989 The Velvet Revolution. The government resigns and is replaced by the dissident-led Civic Forum. Václav Havel is elected president.

1993 Czechoslovakia splits into the independent states of Slovakia and the Czech Republic.

1999 The Czech Republic joins NATO.

2002 Catastrophic floods wreak havoc throughout Prague and the country.

2003 Václav Havel leaves office. Former Prime Minister Václav Klaus is elected to replace him.

WORLD WAR II

In 1938 Britain and France ceded the Sudetenland to Germany, depriving Czechoslovakia of most of its industry and all its defences. The following year, Hitler dismembered the rest of the country and the Czech provinces became the 'Protectorate of Bohemia and Moravia'. In 1942 the assassination of Reichsprotektor Heydrich by Czechoslovak parachutists led to brutal repression by the Nazis.

PRAGUE SPRING

In the 'Prague Spring' of 1968, Czechoslovakia's Communist party, under Alexander Dubček, promised to create 'Socialism with a human face'. Terrified at this prospect, the Soviet Union sent in tanks and took the government off to Moscow in chains. The last Soviet troops left in 1991.

Time to Shop

It's getting increasingly hard for travellers to escape uniformity and find local products worth taking home. Thanks to their long tradition as craftsmen and artisans, however, the Czechs

have plenty to offer visitors. Along with crystal and garnets, don't overlook the herbal liqueur Becherovka, blue onion porcelain and art books.

Antique stores, found under signs reading *starožítnictví*, *bazar* or *vetesnictví* (junk shop), contain many treasures: Quality paintings, kitchenware, jewellery and linens can be found at reasonable prices. Many bazaars specialize in old cameras, clocks and other mechanical devices.

A number of Czech fashion designers are making a name for themselves and have opened successful boutiques where you can find original pieces at a fraction of what you'd pay at home for a similar-quality item. Most of these shops are concentrated on a few streets north of Old Town Square—Dlouhá, Dušní and V Kolkovně. Fashionable international names line nearby Pařížska, but don't expect any bargains there.

Considering the Czechs' contribution to art, architecture and photography, it's not surprising

SPA TREATS

A whole culture has grown up around Czech spa towns. Re-create this atmosphere at home by strolling about, sipping water from a porcelain cup with a built-straw and sipping spa waters, or *oplátky*. The cups can be found cheaply in antique shops. Round off your cure with a shot of Becherovka, the herbal liqueur developed by a spa doctor in Karlovy Vary in 1807. It's said to be especially good for stomach ailments.

that handsome coffee-table books devoted to subjects such as Czech cubism, avant-garde photography and the art-nouveau movement are popular.

Below left: *String puppet on a street vendor's stalls*
Below: *Pirken Hammer porcelain*

Glass and crystal, of course, are ubiquitous, and sometimes the sheer number of shops and variety of products can be overwhelming. But Czech crystal is famous for a reason and should not be overlooked. Stick to shops affiliated with just one or two manufacturers that focus primarily on tableware and larger individual pieces and that don't waste space on knick-knacks, and you're likely to take home something of real quality. Look for hand-blown, hand-cut lead crystal produced by names such as Moser and Sklo Bohemia, and Desná for art deco.

In Prague, as anywhere, let the buyer beware. Much of what is sold in the tourist areas has no relation to local traditions or culture: Russian dolls, Polish amber and non-Czech crystal. Lace tablecloths are more likely to have been made by Russian experts than Czech ones. If any of these products catches your eye and doesn't break the bank there's nothing wrong in buying it—but if your heart is set on a real Czech souvenir, you may want to keep looking.

NOT ALL GARNETS ARE CREATED EQUAL

The Czechs have been mining garnets for centuries. Said to bring vitality and cure depression, the Bohemian variety of garnet is not found anywhere else in the world. The colour is a deep, rich red known as 'dove's blood' and the settings typically feature many small garnets clustered together. Most garnet jewellery is made by the cooperative Granát Turnov and sold in factory stores and by authorized dealers with a stamp of approval. However, a fair amount of what is sold in Prague as Bohemian garnets is actually made from almandines or other stones from Italy and elsewhere. Showy gold pieces set with large, brownish stones are not Bohemian garnets.

Out and About

PIS

✉ Na příkopě 20, Nové Město ☎ 12444 (general information) 🕓 Mon–Fri 9–7, Sat–Sun 9–5 summer; Mon–Fri 9–6, Sat 9–3 winter

🚇 Náměstí Republiky;

✉ Staroměstské náměstí 1 (Old Town Hall)

🕓 Mon–Fri 9–7, Sat–Sun 9–6 summer; Mon–Fri 9–6, Sat–Sun 9–5 winter

🚇 Staroměstská

Čedok

✉ Na příkopě 18, Nové Město ☎ 224 197 111; fax 222 244 421

🚇 Náměstí Republiky or Můstek

Prague Walks

✉ Na příkopě 23, Nové Město ☎ 606 600 123 (mobile)

EVD

✉ Quayside at Čechův most, Staré Město ☎ 224 810 030 🚇 Staroměstská

INFORMATION

HRAD KARLŠTEJN

Distance 35km (21miles)

Journey Time 40 minutes

☎ Reservations: 274 008 154; castle 311 681 617

🕓 Daily 9–5, May–Sep (also until 6 Jul, Aug); 9–4 Apr, Oct; 9–3, Nov–Mar

🚆 Prague–Smíchov to Karlštejn

🎫 Moderate

ORGANIZED SIGHTSEEING

A good starting point for finding out about tours is the official Prague Information Service (Pražská informační služba—PIS). Čedok is the longest-established travel company in Prague. You could also try Premiant City Tour (☎ 224 946 922).

A main starting point for themed walks is Old Town Square; check local posters for starting times. Also try Prague Walks. Walking tours around Prague Castle in the company of a well-informed guide start from the information centre opposite the main doors of St. Vitus's Cathedral. Boat tours along the Vltava range from hour-long trips to lengthier excursions that include a meal. Companies offering boat tours include EVD and Kedršt (☎ 602 619 791).

EXCURSIONS

HRAD KARLŠTEJN (KARLŠTEJN CASTLE)

This mighty fortress, one of the great sights of Bohemia, towers above the glorious woodlands of the gorge of the River Berounka. The superb panorama from the castle walls will compensate you for the climb up. The castle was started in 1348 and its name celebrates the Emperor Charles IV. He conceived it as a sort of sacred bunker, a repository for the Crown Jewels and his collection of holy relics. The castle was also planned as a personal, processional way that the emperor would follow to its climax—the Great Tower containing the Chapel of the Holy Rood.

ZÁMEK KONOPIŠTĚ (KONOPIŠTĚ CASTLE)

Konopiště Castle's round towers rise in romantic fashion above the surrounding woodlands. The palace's origins go back to the 14th century, but it owes its present appearance largely to Archduke Franz Ferdinand, heir to the Habsburg throne,

who acquired it in 1887. The corridors are filled with trophies of the countless wild creatures he slaughtered while waiting for the demise of his long-lived uncle Franz Joseph. The archduke met his own violent end when he was cut down by an assassin's bullet in Sarajevo, triggering the start of World War I. The castle is full of Franz Ferdinand's fine furniture and his collection of weapons. His other obsession was landscape gardening, and the parklands and rose garden are a delight.

MĚLNÍK

Built on a bluff near the confluence of the Vltava and Elbe rivers, this ancient town is famous for the vineyards that rise up in terraces beneath its imposing castle. Following the demise of Communism, Mělník's castle and estates have been returned to the original aristocratic Lobkovic owners. Long before the Lobkovic family, however, it was a royal seat, abode of the Czech queens, one of whom raised her grandson Wenceslas (later the 'Good King') here. The castle courtyard, with its Gothic and Renaissance wings and ancient wine cellars, is approached via the charmingly arcaded town square.

Far left: *Karlstein Castle*
Centre: *Church of Sts Peter and Paul, Melnik*

INFORMATION

ZÁMEK KONOPIŠTĚ
Distance 43km (26 miles)
Journey Time 45 minutes by car; one hour by train then short distance by local bus or taxi
✉ Zámek Konopiště, Benešov u Prahy
☎ 317 721 336
🕐 Tue–Sun 9–12, 1–5, May–Aug; 9–12, 1–4, Sep; 9–12, 1–3, Apr–Oct
🚆 Train to Benešov from Hlavní nádraží (1 hour) then bus or taxi
✋ Moderate

Above left: *Bronze sculpture at the entrance to Konopiste Castle, summer residence of the ill-fated Archduke Franz Ferdinand*

INFORMATION

MĚLNÍK
Distance 30km (18 miles)
Journey Time 50 minutes
✉ Svatováclavská, Mělník
☎ 315 622 108
🕐 Daily 10–5, Mar–Dec. Winter check locally
🚌 Bus from Nádraží Holešovice Metro/bus/ train station
✋ Moderate

21

Walks

THE SIGHTS

- Old Town Hall (➤ 44)
- Clam-Gallas Palace
- Old Town Bridge Tower (➤ 37)
- Karlův most (Charles Bridge, ➤ 37)
- Chrám sv Mikuláše (St. Nicholas's Church, ➤ 35)
- Nerudova (➤ 34)

INFORMATION

Distance 2km (1.2 miles)
Time 1 hour
Start point ★
Staroměstské náměstí (Old Town Square)
⊞ E4
🚇 Staroměstská
End point Hradčanské náměstí (Hradčany Square)
⊞ C4
🚋 Tram 22, 23

Below: *Crossing Charles Bridge*

IN THE FOOTSTEPS OF KINGS—THE OLD TOWN TO THE CASTLE

This walk follows the Royal Way, the ancient coronation route taken by Czech kings from their city centre residence to the cathedral high up in Hradčany. It starts in Staroměstské náměstí (Old Town Square) and is popular, so you are likely to have plenty of company.

Go west into Malé náměstí (Little Square), with its delightful fountain, and turn into twisting Karlova Street, with its tempting gift shops. The street's final curve brings you into Křižovnické náměstí (Knights of the Cross Square). Look out for the traffic as you rush to enjoy the incomparable view of the castle across the river.

Pass through the Old Town Bridge Tower onto Karlův most (Charles Bridge); admire the stunning procession of saintly statues. As it approaches Malá Strana, the bridge becomes a flyover, then, after the Malá Strana Bridge Tower, it leads you to Mostecká (Bridge) Street. Cross Malostranské náměstí (Malá Strana Square), dominated by the great bulk of Chrám sv. Mikuláše (St. Nicholas' Church), with care. Grit your teeth in preparation for the climb up Nerudova, and don't forget to turn sharp right onto the final leg of the castle approach, Ke hradu. Regain your breath while leaning on the wall of Hradčanské náměstí (Hradčany Square) and soak up the panorama of the city far below, a just reward for the climb.

BACK TO THE OLD TOWN VIA SOME OF PRAGUE'S GARDENS

From Hradčanské náměstí walk up Loretánská Street, making a U-turn left as you enter Pohořelec Square. A short way down Úvoz, make a sharp right and stop to enjoy the view from the vineyard lying just below Strahovský klášter (Strahov Monastery). The vineyard is a leftover from the days when vines clad most of the slopes hereabouts. Go through the monastery courtyard, turning right into Pohořelec, then left into Loretánské náměstí. Černínská Street leads downhill into Nový Svět.

Return to Hradčanské náměstí via Nový Svět and Kanovnická. Go through the Matthias Gate of the castle, then out of the north gate from the castle's Second Courtyard. Turn into the Královská zahrada (Royal Gardens); leave them near the Belvedere summer palace and enter the Chotkovy sady (Chotek Gardens). Cross the footbridge into Letenské sady (Letná Plain), and view the city from the Hanavský pavilon, then from the plinth where Stalin's statue stood. Descend the steps and ramps to the Čechův most (Čech Bridge) and return to Staroměstské náměstí via Josefov—the former Jewish ghetto.

Above: *The entrance gates into the courtyard of Prague Castle*

23

Prague by Night

Left to right: Prague Castle at night; chess is popular in Czeckoslavakia; jazz entertainers in a Prague bar

WHAT'S ON

The best source of information for English readers about what's on in Prague is probably the tabloid 'Night and Day' section of the weekly English-language newspaper *Prague Post*. This gives listings of stage, screen and cultural events likely to be relevant to visitors from abroad, as well as reviews, comment and analysis. Listings can also be found in the free biweekly *Prague Pill*. Tickets for events can be obtained at individual box offices (which may be cheaper) or through PIS (➤ 20); Ticketpro (☎ 296 329 999); or Bohemia Ticket International (☎ 224 227 832).

DRINKING IN PRAGUE

Prague has no shortage of hip dance clubs and trendy bars, but for most Czechs, the best nights are spent in a pub. No visitor should pass up the opportunity to savour an expertly poured Pilsner or Budvar at the long wooden tables of a typical Czech pub. Wine bars sometimes come in the guise of a restaurant, but the true *vinára* is a small establishment, sometimes with standing room only, that offers Moravian, Bohemian or Slovak wines, often from the barrel, along with light cold snacks. These wines can be surprisingly good and are usually quite inexpensive.

ALL THAT JAZZ

Czechs are known for being a musical nation and on any given night there are a variety of concerts on offer, from local modern jazz fixtures like Emil Viklický to touring Balkan gypsy bands to performances of Dvořák and Smetana. Postage-stamp jazz joints abound in the centre and larger venues like Malostranská beseda, the Roxy and Akropolis book an eclectic mix of acts.

STAYING OUT LATE

Until fairly recently Prague closed up shop at 10pm, and in the residential areas pubs and restaurants still tend to shut down fairly early, as many people start work at 7 or 8am. Night owls thirsty for a cocktail should head for the bars just north of Old Town Square. Another district that's home to hip bars and clubs is located behind the National Theatre. Of course you can always take a romantic stroll and view the floodlit castle from the blissfully empty Charles Bridge.

PRAGUE's
top 25 sights

The sights are shown on the maps on the inside front cover and inside back cover, numbered **1**–**25** from west to east across the city

Strahovský klášter

Baroque spires rising towards Heaven, a gilded image of an enemy of the Faith, monks profiting from an enterprise in Hell: The Strahov Monastery seems to encapsulate something of this most paradoxical of cities.

Persuasive priests The Strahov Monastery, a major landmark in the cityscape, crowns the steep slope leading up from Malá Strana (its name derives from *strahovní*, meaning 'to watch over'). It is a treasure-house of literature, and its ornate library halls with their splendid frescos are among the most magnificent in Europe. As befits a monastery devoted to books, Strahov owed much to its abbots' way with words. Its 12th-century founder, Abbot Zdík, persuaded Prince Vladislav II to back his project by making flattering comparisons of Prague with the holy city of Jerusalem. Much later, in 1783, Abbot Meyer exercised equal powers of persuasion on Emperor Joseph II to exempt Strahov from the reforming ruler's edict that closed down many of the Habsburg Empire's monasteries. The canny cleric was so eloquent that Strahov actually benefited from the misfortune of other institutions: Books from the suppressed monastery at Louka were brought here by the wagonload. A gilded medallion of the emperor over the library entrance may also have helped to persuade Joseph that the Strahov monks deserved special treatment.

Returnees' revenge The monks, who belong to the Premonstratensian Order, were chased out of Strahov by the Communists in 1952, but have now come back. They have made the upper floor of the cloisters into a gallery for the works of art since returned to them and converted the cellars into a restaurant called Peklo (Hell).

Nový Svět

Chambermaids and scullions, footmen and flunkies—these were among the folk for whom the humble homes of Nový Svět ('New World') were erected back in the 14th century. The area is now more upmarket.

Wizards and weird doings Nový Svět, a mysterious place of crooked alleyways and secret gardens hidden behind high walls, has never been in the city's mainstream. Castle servants lived here. So did intellectuals and others who served the masters of the castle—the Danish astronomer Tycho Brahe and his German colleague Johannes Kepler, both employed by Rudolph II to investigate the more arcane secrets of the universe.

La Bohème Today's residents are artists and writers, who have colonized the 18th-century houses along this charming cobbled street that wobbles its way westward just uphill from the castle. The painter's studio at No. 19 is crammed with pictures of curvaceous girls and grimacing gnomes, while the Czech master of animated film, Jan Švankmajer, a long-time resident, runs a gallery devoted to Surrealist art.

Connecting the worlds Nový Svět is linked to the outside world by short streets (Černínská, Kapucínská, U Kasáren and Kanovnická) that run down the hill from the main tourist trail between Strahovský klášter and the castle, and by flights of steps that lead from the old ramparts, whose course is followed by today's trams 22 and 23.

HIGHLIGHTS

- Nepomuk statue in Černínská Street
- Birthplace of violinist F Ondříček at No. 25
- Tycho Brahe's house at No. 1
- Church of St. John Nepomuk
- No. 3, former President Havel's favourite restaurant (➤ 65)

INFORMATION

- C4: Locator map A2
- Nový Svět, Hradčany
- Restaurant at No. 3
- Tram 22, 23 to Brusnice
- Few
- Loretánská kaple (Loreto Shrine, ➤ 26)

St. John Nepomuk

Loretánská kaple

HIGHLIGHTS

- The main façade, with statuary and carillon
- The Santa Casa
- Interior of the Church of the Nativity
- Diamond monstrance in the Loreto Treasure
- Cloister painting of St. Starosta

Loreto Shrine, Hradčany

INFORMATION

- C4: Locator map A2
- Loretánské náměstí, Hradčany
- 220 516 740
- Tue–Sun 9–12.15, 1–4.30
- Tram 22, 23 to Pohořelec
- Few
- Moderate
- Strahov Monastery (► 26), Nový Svět (► 27)

A bearded lady, skeletons rattling their bones to the sound of chiming bells, severed breasts and a flying house are not part of a freak show, but instead are all features of the sumptuous Loreto Shrine, on Hradčany Hill.

Counter-Reformation fireworks No showman's trick was spared to bring the wayward Czechs back into the Catholic fold after their long flirtation with Protestantism was brought to an end by the Battle of the White Mountain in 1620. Protestant austerity, with its repudiation of images, was replaced by the idolatry of the cult of the Virgin Mary, dripping with sensuality and symbolism. Of all the flights of architectural fantasy that the Roman Catholic Counter-Reformation perpetrated on Prague, the Loreto is the most bizarre as well as the most beautiful, its church and courtyard a theatre of cults, miracles and mysteries designed to dazzle doubters and sceptics.

Weird wonders The kernel of the complex is a Santa Casa, a facsimile of the Virgin Mary's holy home in Nazareth, supposedly flown by angels from the Holy Land and deposited at Loreto in Italy. Fifty such shrines were once scattered around the Czech countryside, but this is far and away the most important, an ornate little Renaissance pavilion built in 1631 and later given an equally ornate baroque setting of courtyard, carillon tower and richly decorated church. Pilgrims once flocked here in huge numbers to marvel at the macabre: St. Agatha offering up her bloody bosom to the angels; the skeletons in their wax death masks; unhappy St. Starosta, whose father killed her in a fury on finding she'd grown a beard to discourage a favoured suitor.

Šternberský palác

Who would guess that the little alley beside the Prague archbishop's palace would lead to one of the nation's great art collections? Housed in the grand Šternberg Palace, it dazzles visitors with its Old Masters.

Ambitious aristocrats Having built the Trojský zámek (Troja Château ►50) on the edge of Prague, Count Šternberg, one of the city's richest men, needed a town house closer to Prague Castle. The Italian architect Giovanni Alliprandi was commissioned to design the palace, and work began on the count's Hradčany home in 1698. However, the money ran out before the completion of the main façade, the principal purpose of which was to upstage his neighbour, the archbishop. The interior was decorated with fine ceiling and wall paintings. It was a later Šternberg who donated much of the family's great picture collection to the precursor to the National Gallery in the early 19th century, and the nation's finest foreign paintings were housed here from 1821 to 1871. They are once more in this grand setting.

Picture palace Despite being tucked away behind Hradčanské náměstí, the Šternberg Palace is an edifice of some substance, arranged around an imposing courtyard, with grand stairways and an oval pavilion facing the garden. The National Gallery of European Art attracts a stream of tourists—as well as art thieves, tempted by security that was laughably lax until it was tightened up not long ago. The pictures could keep an art lover busy for a whole day or more, though some star exhibits are no longer on view: A policy of restitution has returned them to the owners from whom they were confiscated by the Communists.

HIGHLIGHTS

- Triptych of the Adoration of the Magi, Giertgen tot Sint Jans
- *Adam and Eve*, Cranach
- *Feast of the Rosary*, Dürer
- *Scholar in his Study*, Rembrandt
- *Head of Christ*, El Greco
- Portraits from 2nd-century Egypt
- *Beheading of St Dorothy*, Hans Baldung Grien
- *Eleonora of Toledo*, Bronzino
- *St. Jerome*, Ribera

INFORMATION

- ✠ C4: Locator map B2
- ✉ Hradčanské náměstí, Hradčany
- ☎ 233 090 570
- 🕐 Tue–Sun 10–6
- 🍴 Café
- 🚊 Tram 22, 23 to Pražský hrad
- ♿ Few
- 💰 Moderate
- 🔗 Pražský hrad (Prague Castle ►31) Military Museum, Schwarzenberský palác (►56)

Top: Big Lunch, painted by Georg Flegel in 1638

Petřín

- Rozhledna viewing tower
- 14th-century Hunger Wall
- Mirror Maze (Bludiště)
- Charles Bridge Battle diorama
- Observatory and Planetarium
- Rose Garden
- Alpine Garden
- Baroque Kostel sv Vavřince (Church of St. Lawrence)
- Křížová cesta (Calvary Chapel and Stations of the Cross)
- Ukranian timber Kostel sv Michala (Church of St. Michael)

INFORMATION

- ✚ C–D4–5: Locator map B2
- ⊙ Rozhledna, Mirror Maze: daily 10–7, Apr–Aug; 10–6, Sep–Oct.; Sat–Sun 10–5, rest of year. Observatory hours vary; for information call PIS (☎ 12444)
- ⚑ Restaurant and café
- ⚑ Funicular railway, from Újezd in Malá Strana
- ⊡ Tram 22, 23 to Pohořelec then walk
- ⚑ Few
- ⚑ Rozhledna, Mirror Maze, Observatory: inexpensive
- ⟷ Strahovský klášter (Strahov Monastery, ► 26)

When the crowds on Charles Bridge become too much and the pavements become too hard, there's always the glorious green of Petřín Hill, its orchards and woodlands a cool retreat from the city centre—and a real breath of the countryside in the metropolis.

A train with a view In 1891, for the city's great Jubilee Expo that celebrated the achievements of the Czech provinces when they still formed part of the Austrian Empire, the city fathers provided a jolly little funicular railway (the 'Lanovka') to the top of Petřín Hill. Now restored, it once again carries passengers effortlessly up the steep slope. At the top there's a whole array of attractions, including the Rozhledna ('Lookout'), the little brother of the Eiffel Tower, also built in 1891. Its 299 steps lead to a viewing platform; some claim to have seen, on a clear day, not only the Czech Republic's Giant Mountains, 145km (90 miles) to the northeast, but also the Alps, even farther away to the southwest. And all of Prague is at your feet.

Country matters With its woods and orchards (splendid with blossom in spring), Petřín provides a welcome counterpoint to the busy castle area. Once there were vineyards on the

hill, but these didn't survive the Thirty Years War in the 17th century. They were replaced by the superb gardens that link the palaces of Malá Strana to the surrounding hillside parklands.

Pražský hrad

The thousand windows of Prague Castle gaze down into every corner of the city. This is the citadel of the Czech nation, holder of its collective memory. It is a place of palaces, churches, streets and squares, sheltering some of the country's greatest treasures.

Age-old stronghold The princes of Prague first built a fortress on the limestone spur high above the Vltava in the 9th century, and the Czech provinces have been ruled from here ever since (except when rulers preferred to live in a long-vanished palace in the city centre or on the summit of the rock upstream at Vyšehrad). Every age has left its imprint on the castle; it is a storehouse of architectural styles, ranging from the foundations of Romanesque churches a thousand years old to Professor Plečnik's premature postmodernism of the interwar years. Even now, a committee is hard at work adapting the ancient complex in an attempt to make it more inviting and accessible to the citizens of a new and democratic order.

Castle denizens Teeming with tourists, the castle's courtyards also echo with the tread of countless ghosts: Emperor Charles IV, with his dreams of Prague as a great imperial capital; the cranky Habsburg ruler Rudolph II, attended by his retinue of alchemists and necromancers, soothsayers and erotic painters; the Protestant mob that flung the hated Catholic councillors down from the Chancellery windows; Tomáš Garringue Masaryk, philosopher-president and father of Czechoslovakia; Adolf Hitler *Heil*-ing his hysterical helots; and, most recently, the Communists, enjoying their privileges while they lasted.

HIGHLIGHTS

- Giants guarding the western gateway
- Mihulka Tower
- Vladislav Hall in Old Royal Palace
- Tiny houses in Golden Lane
- Lobkovic Palace (Czech History Museum)
- Outline of Matthias Gate in First Courtyard
- Second Courtyard, with Holy Rood Chapel and the Picture Gallery
- Third Courtyard, with statue of St George
- Plečnik's canopy and stairway to gardens
- Riders' Staircase in Old Royal Palace

INFORMATION

- C–D4: Locator map B2
- Pražský hrad, Hradčany
- 224 373 368
- Courtyards and street: daily until late. Buildings: daily 9–5, Apr–Oct; 9–4, rest of year
- Cafés and restaurants
- Malostranská, then an uphill walk
- Tram 22, 23 to Pražský hrad
- Few
- Moderate
- Šternberský palác (▶ 29), Katedrála sv Víta (St. Vitus's Cathedral, ▶ 32)

Katedrála sv Víta

HIGHLIGHTS

- South Portal, with 14th-century mosaic
- St. Wenceslas's Chapel
- Crypt, with royal tombs
- Silver tomb of St. John Nepomuk
- West front sculptures

INFORMATION

- ✚ C/D4: Locator map B2
- ✉ Pražský hrad, Hradčany
- 🕓 Daily 9–5, Apr–Oct; 9–4, rest of year. Tower: daily 10–5, Apr–Oct
- 🍴 Restaurants and cafés in castle
- 🚊 Tram 22, 23 to Pražský hrad (Prague Castle)
- ♿ Fair
- 🎫 Newer section: free. Gothic section: moderate
- ⮕ Pražský hrad (➤ 31)

Tomb of St. John Nepomuk

To emerge into Prague Castle's Third Courtyard and see the twin towers of St. Vitus's Cathedral lancing skyward is truly breathtaking. The sight is all the more compelling when you realize that this Gothic edifice was completed within living memory.

Spanning the centuries The cathedral was begun by Emperor Charles IV in the mid-14th century. It is built over the foundations of much earlier predecessors: a round church erected by 'Good King' (actually Prince) Wenceslas in the early 10th century and a big Romanesque building resembling the present-day Bazilika sv Jiří (➤ 33). The glory of the architecture is largely due to the great Swabian builder Petr Parléř and his sons, who worked on the building for 60 years. Progress was halted abruptly by the troubles of the 15th century, and the cathedral consisted only of an east end until the formation of an 'Association for the Completion of the Cathedral', in 1843. Decades of effort saw the nave, western towers and much else brought to a triumphant conclusion; in 1929, a thousand years after Prince Wenceslas was assassinated, the cathedral was consecrated, dedicated to the country's patron saint, St. Vitus.

Cathedral treasures The cathedral is a treasure house of Bohemian history, though the Crown Jewels, its greatest prize, are seldom on display. The spacious interior absorbs the crowds with ease and provides a fitting context for an array of precious artefacts that range from medieval paintings to modern glass.

Bazilika a klášter sv Jiří

A blood-red baroque façade conceals a severe ancient interior, the Romanesque Basilica of St. George. The nuns have long since left their convent to the north, which is now a setting for fine collections of Czech Renaissance and baroque painting and sculpture.

Bare basilica The basilica is the biggest church of its date in the Czech provinces and its twin towers and pale, sober stonework are a reminder of the great antiquity of the Prague Castle complex. Very well preserved, it is no longer used as a church but is instead a concert venue. The austere interior, a great hall with wooden ceiling, houses a small but impressive collection of artworks.

Paintings and princesses Founded in 973, St. George's Convent was a prestigious institution, a place to which princesses and other young ladies of noble birth were sent to receive the best possible education. Shut down like many other religious houses in 1782 by Emperor Joseph (who turned it into a barracks), it had to await the coming of the Communists for its rehabilitation; they planned to turn it into a Museum of the Czechoslovak People. It now houses Mannerist, baroque and rococo painting and sculpture from the National Gallery's Old Bohemian collection. The comparatively small Mannerist holdings complement those at the Obrazárna (the Prague Castle Picture Gallery ► 54). The finest artworks here represent the Bohemian baroque, which flowered at a time when Czechs were allowed few creative outlets other than the visual arts. Massive sculpted saints writhe in ecstatic frenzy. Meanwhile, secular portraits and genre scenes illustrate other sides of Bohemian life.

HIGHLIGHTS

Basilica
- Gothic tomb of Prince Vratislav I
- St. Ludmila's chapel with frescos
- Renaissance south portal

Gallery
- Baroque Annunciation sculptures from East Bohemia
- Religious statuary by Jiří František Pacák and M. B. Braun
- *Tobias Restoring his Father's Sight* by Petr Brandl
- Landscapes by Roelandt Savery
- Genre scenes by Norbert Grund

INFORMATION

- D4: Locator map B2
- Jiřské náměstí, Hradčany
- 257 320 536
- Basilica: daily 9–5, Apr–Oct; 9–4, rest of year Gallery: Tue–Sun 10–6
- Restaurants and cafés in castle
- Malostranská, then an uphill walk
- Tram 22, 23 to Pražský hrad (Prague Castle)
- Few
- Moderate
- Pražský hrad (► 31)

Nerudova

HIGHLIGHTS

- No. 2, U kocoura (The Tomcat) pub
- No. 5, Morzin Palace
- No. 6, The Red Eagle
- No. 12, The Three Little Fiddles
- No. 16, The Golden Goblet
- No. 20, Thun-Hohenstein Palace
- No. 27, The Golden Key
- No. 34, The Golden Horseshoe
- Baroque Church of Our Lady of Divine Providence
- No. 47, The Two Suns, home of Jan Neruda

INFORMATION

- ✚ C–D4: Locator map B2
- ✉ Nerudova, Malá Strana
- 🍴 Restaurants and cafés
- 🚊 Trams 12, 22, 23 to Malostranské náměstí (Malá Strana Square)
- ♿ Few
- ↔ Pražský hrad (Prague Castle ➤ 31)
  Chrám sv Mikuláše (St. Nicholas's Church), Malá Strana (➤ 35)

Toil up to the castle from Malá Strana Square via steep, cobbled Neruda Street and be rewarded by a sequence of exquisite baroque and rococo town houses, on medieval foundations, with elaborate house signs.

Eagles and other emblems It is the elegant façades and their emblems that catch the eye. There's an Eagle, Three Little Fiddles, a Goblet, a Golden Key and a Horseshoe. The Two Suns indicate the house (No. 47) of author Jan Neruda (1834–91), who gave his name to the street; he was the Dickens of Malá Strana, a shrewd observer of the everyday life of the area. Most of the people who lived here were prosperous burghers, but some were aristocrats, like the Morzins who built their palace at No. 5 (the muscular Moors holding up the balcony are a pun on the family name). Their home is now an embassy, as is the Thun-Hohensteins' Palace at No. 20; here the Moors' job is being carried out by a pair of odd-looking eagles.

Spur Street The secret of savouring Neruda Street to the full is to coast gently downward, like the coachmen from whom the road derived its earlier German name of Spornergasse (Spur Street), the spur in this case being the skid-like brake that slowed their otherwise precipitous progress down the steep slope.

The Three Little Fiddles, No. 12 Nerudova

Chrám sv Mikuláše, Malá Strana

As you crawl insect-like around the base of the lofty St. Nicholas's Church, you feel the full power of the Catholic Counter-Reformation expressing itself in one of the boldest, most beautiful baroque buildings of Central Europe.

Counter-Reformation citadel When the Jesuits came to Prague following the rout of the Protestants at the Battle of the White Mountain, the existing little 13th-century church at the centre of Malostranské náměstí (Malá Strana Square) was far too modest for their aspirations. The new St. Nicholas's Church was eventually completed in the 18th century and, with its lofty walls and high dome and bell tower, became one of the dominant features of the city. The Jesuits intended their church to impress, but not through size alone. They employed the finest architects of the day (the Dientzenhofers, father and son, plus Anselmo Lurago), along with the most talented interior designers. The subtly undulating west front is adorned with statues proclaiming the triumph of the Jesuit Order under the patronage of the imperial House of Habsburg. Inside, no effort was spared to enthral via the dynamic play of space, statuary and painting, a fantastically decorated pulpit and a 2,500-pipe organ (played by Mozart on several occasions).

Princely palaces and humbler households In front of the huge church swirls the life of Malá Strana—locals waiting for the trams mixing with tourists following the Royal Way (➤ 22) up to Hradčany. Malostranské náměstí is lined with a fascinating mixture of ancient town houses and grand palaces, while attached to St. Nicholas's is the Jesuits's college, now part of the university.

HIGHLIGHTS

Chrám sv Mikuláše
- West front
- St. Barbara's Chapel
- Organ with fresco of St. Cecilia
- Dome with Holy Trinity fresco
- Huge sculptures of four Church Fathers
- Trompe-l'oeil ceiling fresco by Kracker

Malostranské náměstí
- Arcaded houses
- No. 10, Renaissance house
- No. 13, Lichtenstejnský palác of 1791
- Nos. 18 and 19, Smiřický Palace and Šternberg House

INFORMATION

- ✠ D4: Locator map B2
- ✉ Malostranské náměstí
- 🕐 Daily 9–5, Apr–Sep; 9–4, rest of year
- 🍴 Restaurants and cafés in square
- Ⓜ Malostranská
- 🚃 Tram 12, 22, 23 to Malostranské náměstí
- ♿ Few
- 💷 Inexpensive
- ↔ Nerudova (➤ 34), Valdstejnský palác (➤ 36), Karlův most (Charles Bridge, ➤ 37)

Valdštejnský palác

HIGHLIGHTS

- Sala Terrena
- Garden sculptures (copies of originals by de Vries)
- Grotesquery and aviary in garden
- Riding School (gallery with temporary exhibitions)

INFORMATION

➕ D4: Locator map C2
✉ Palace: Valdštejnské náměstí, Malá Strana. Garden: Letenská 10. Riding School: Valdštejnská at Klárov
🕐 Palace: check locally. Garden: daily 9–7, May–Sep; 10–6, late Mar to Apr, Oct. Riding School: Tue–Sun 10–6
🚇 Malostranská
♿ Fair
💰 Garden free
🔁 Nerudova (➤ 34)
Chrám sv Mikuláše (St. Nicholas's Church), Malá Strana (➤ 35)

Think of Wallenstein Palace—Prague's biggest palace—as an awful warning to eschew the excessive ambition and arrogance of its builder, Albrecht von Wallenstein, whose desire for power and fame led to his assassination.

Greedy generalissimo Wallenstein's huge late Renaissance/early baroque palace crouches at the foot of Prague Castle as if waiting greedily to gobble it up. A whole city block, previously occupied by a couple of dozen houses and a brickworks, was demolished to make way for the complex of five courtyards, a barracks, a riding school and a superb garden that were intended to reflect Wallenstein's wealth and status. Wallenstein (Valdštejn in Czech) turned the troubled early 17th century to his advantage. Having wormed his way into the emperor's favour, he became governor of Prague, then duke of Friedland. He married for money (twice), and great tracts of land (even whole towns) fell into his hands following the Battle of the White Mountain in 1620. His fortune grew further as he quartermastered the imperial armies as well as leading them. Rightly suspicious of his subject's intentions—Wallenstein was negotiating with the enemy at the time—the emperor had him killed.

The general's garden The great hall of the palace, with its ceiling painting of Wallenstein as Mars, the god of war, can only be seen if you have friends in the Czech Senate, which now occupies the building. The formal garden is more freely accessible. The latter is dominated by the superb Sala Terrena loggia, modelled on those in Italy, and has convincing copies of the statues stolen by Swedish soldiers during the Thirty Years War.

Karlův most

Any time is right to visit Charles Bridge, the magnificent medieval crossing over the Vltava. Enjoy the hucksters, then savour the almost sinister dusk, when sculpted saints on the parapets gesticulate against the darkening sky.

Gothic overpass For centuries Karlův most was Prague's only bridge, built on the orders of Emperor Charles IV in the 14th century. It's a triumph of Gothic engineering, with 16 massive sandstone arches carrying it more than 490m from the Old Town to soar across the Vltava River and Kampa Island to touch down near the heart of Malá Strana. It is protected by sturdy timber cutwaters and guarded at both ends by towers; the eastern face of the Old Town Bridge Tower is richly ornamented. Its opposite number is accompanied by a smaller tower, once part of the earlier Judith Bridge.

Starry saint Charles Bridge has always been much more than a river crossing. Today's traders succeed earlier merchants and stallholders, and tournaments, battles and executions have all been held on the bridge. The heads of the Protestants executed in 1621 in Old Town Square were displayed here. Later that century the bridge was beautified with baroque sculptures, including the statue of St. John Nepomuk. Falling foul of the king, this unfortunate cleric was pushed off the bridge in a sack. As his body bobbed in the water, five stars danced on the surface. Nepomuk hence became the patron saint of bridges, and is always depicted with his starry halo.

HIGHLIGHTS

- Old Town Bridge Tower
- Malá Strana Bridge Tower (viewpoint)
- Nepomuk statue with bronze relief panels
- Bruncvík (Roland column) to southwest
- Statue of St. John of Matha
- Bronze crucifix with Hebrew inscription
- Statue of St. Luitgard (by Braun)

INFORMATION

- D4: Locator map C2
- Staroměstská
- Tram 12, 22, 23 to Malostranské náměstí
- Good
- Bridge free
- Chrám sv Mikuláše (St. Nicholas's Church), Malá Strana (▶ 35)

St. Anthony of Padua

Národní divadlo

- Bronze troikas above the entrance loggia
- Star-patterned roof of the dome
- Frescos in the foyer by Mikoláš Aleš
- Painted ceiling of the auditorium, by František Ženíšek
- Painted stage curtain by Vojtěch Hynais
- View of the theatre from Střelecký Island
- Any performance of an opera from the Czech repertoire

INFORMATION

- D/E5: Locator map C3
- Národní 2, Nové Město
- 224 901 448
- Bar
- Tram 6, 9, 18, 21, 22, 23 to Národní divadlo
- Few
- Opera tickets: Kč40–900
- Betlémská kaple (► 57)

A reflection of the National Theatre

Even if the thought of a classical play performed in Czech doesn't enthrall you, don't miss the National Theatre. It is, perhaps, the greatest of Prague's collective works of art, decorated by the finest artists of the age.

National drama Theatre in Prague still spoke with a German voice in the mid-19th century. Money to build a specifically Czech theatre was collected from 1849 onward, without support from German-dominated officialdom. The foundation stone was laid in 1868 with much festivity, then in 1881, just before the first performance, the theatre burnt down. Undiscouraged, the populace rallied, and by 1883 it had been completely rebuilt. The opening was celebrated with a grand gala performance of the opera *Libuše* by Smetana, a passionate supporter of the theatre project.

Expanded ambition The National Theatre stands at the New Town end of Most Legií (Legions Bridge), its bulk carefully angled to fit into the streetscape and not diminish the view to Petřín Hill on the far bank. It was given a long-deserved restoration in time for its centenary, and when it reopened in 1983 it had gained a piazza and three annexes, whose architecture has been much maligned, the least unkind comment being that the buildings seem to be clad in bubble-wrap. Prague's highly popular multimedia show Laterna Magika (► 81) performs in one of these buildings, the Nová scéna.

Uměleckoprůmyslové muzeum

Don't be put off by the uninviting building or the forlornly flapping banner of the Decorative Arts Museum. A steep flight of stairs leads to treasure chambers full of fine furniture, glass, porcelain, clocks and more.

Riverside reclaimed Looking something like a miniature Louvre, the Decorative Arts Museum was built in 1901 in an area that, by the end of the 19th century, had turned its back on the river and become a jumble of storage depots and timber yards. The city fathers decided to beautify it with fine public buildings and riverside promenades on the Parisian model. The School of Arts and Crafts (1884) and the Rudolfinum concert hall and gallery (1890) preceded the museum; the University's Philosophy Building (1929), which completed the enclosure of what is now Jan Palach Square, followed it.

Decorative delights The museum's collections are incredibly rich and diverse, numbering nearly 200,000 items of international origin. Unfortunately only a fraction has ever been on display at any one time. The focus is on beautiful objects originating in the Czech provinces and dating from Renaissance times to the middle of the 20th century. Totally revamped displays now reveal the collections in a fascinating new light.

The 20th century The extraordinary Czech contribution to the development of 20th-century art and design has never been dealt with adequately, a situation that has been partly remedied by the opening of the Museum of Modern Art at Veletržní palác (▶ 49) in 1995.

HIGHLIGHTS

- *Pietra dura* scene of a town by Castnicci
- Beer glasses engraved with card players
- Boulle commode and cabinet
- Monumental baroque furniture by Dientzenhofer and Santini
- Meissen Turk on a rhino
- Holíc porcelain figures
- Harrachov glass
- Klášterec figurines of Prague characters
- Biedermeier cradle
- Surprise view down into the Old Jewish Cemetery

INFORMATION

- ✚ E4: Locator map C2
- ✉ 17 listopadu 2, Staré Město
- ☎ 224 811 241
- 🕐 Tue–Sun 10–6
- 🍴 Café (🕐 Mon–Fri 10–6; Sat–Sun 10.30–6)
- Ⓜ Staroměstská
- ♿ Few
- 💷 Moderate
- ↔ Staronová synagóga, Josefov (▶ 41)
  Starý židovský hřbitov (Old Jewish Cemetery, ▶ 42)

39

Vyšehrad

HIGHLIGHTS

- National Cemetery graves and memorials and the Slavín mausoleum
- St. Martin's Rotunda (Romanesque church)
- Cihelná brána (Brick Gate), with Prague Fortifications Museum
- Baroque Leopold Gate
- Ramparts walk
- Neo-Gothic Kostel sv Petra a Pavla (Church of St. Peter and St. Paul)
- Freestanding sculptures of Libuše and other legendary figures (by Josef Václav Myslbek)

INFORMATION

- E7: Locator map D4
- Information centre: V Pevnosti, Vyšehrad. Brick Gate: Vratislavova, Vyšehrad
- Prague Fortifications Museum: daily 9.30–5.30, Apr–Oct; 9.30–4.30, rest of year. Cemetery: daily 8–6, Apr–Oct; 8–4, rest of year
- Restaurant
- Vyšehrad
- Trams 3, 16, 17, 21 to Výtoň then a steep uphill walk
- Fair
- Park and cemetery: free. Museum: inexpensive
- Congress centre, Vyšehrad (▶ 53)

Rising high above the River Vltava is Vyšehrad ('High Castle'), where the soothsaying Princess Libuše foresaw the founding of Prague, and where she married her ploughman swain, Přemysl.

Romantic rock Beneath Vyšehrad's 19th-century neo-Gothic Church of St. Peter and St. Paul are the remains of a far earlier, Romanesque church that once served the royal court. But it was in the 19th century, with the rise of Romantic ideas about history and nationhood, that poets, playwrights and painters celebrated the great fortress-rock, elaborating the story of Libuše. Most of their efforts have been forgotten, though Smetana's 'Vyšehrad', part of his glorious tone-poem *Má Vlast* remains popular.

Devil's Pillars, Karlach's Park

The nation's great and good have been buried in the National Cemetery (or Pantheon) at Vyšehrad since the late 19th century. Smetana himself is here, and fellow composer Dvořák.

Vltava views Everyone driving along the main riverside highway has to pay homage to Vyšehrad, as the road and tram tracks twist and turn and then tunnel through the high rock protruding into the Vltava. In the 1920s the whole hilltop was turned into a public park, with wonderful views up and down the river (▶ 53).

Staronová synagóga, Josefov

To step down from the street through the low portal of Josefov's Old/New Synagogue is to enter another world, one that endured a thousand years until brought to a tragic end by the brutal Nazi occupation.

Ghetto memories The Old/New Synagogue stands in the heart of Josefov, the former Jewish Ghetto. Prague's Jews moved here in the 13th century; by that time they had already lived at various locations in the city for hundreds of years. High walls kept the Jews in and their Christian neighbours out, though not in 1389, when 3,000 Jews died in a vicious pogrom and the synagogue's floor ran with blood. The ghetto community produced some remarkable characters, such as Rabbi Loew—Renaissance scholar, confidant of emperors and creator of that archetypal man-made monster, the Golem. Moulded from river mud, the mournful Golem first served his master dutifully, but eventually ran amok until the rabbi managed to calm him down. Legend has it that the monster's remains are hidden in the synagogue's loft. Far worse monsters marched in as the Germans annexed Czechoslovakia in 1939; by the end of World War II most of the country's Jews had perished, some in the Czech prison town of Terezín (Theresienstadt), the majority in Auschwitz.

Gothic synagogue With its pointed brick gable and atmospheric interior, the Gothic Old/New Synagogue of 1275 is the oldest building of its kind north of the Alps, a compelling reminder of the age-old intertwining of Jewish and Christian culture in Europe. It is at its most evocative when least crowded with visitors. Remember that for Prague's few remaining Jews it is not a museum but still a place of worship.

HIGHLIGHTS

- Vine carving in entrance portal
- Unconventional five-ribbed vaults
- Gothic grille of the *bimah* (pulpit)
- Rabbi Loew's seat
- Imperial banner recognizing Jewish bravery in the Thirty Years War
- Ark with foliage carving

INFORMATION

- E4: Locator map D2
- Pařížská and Červená
- Sun–Thu 9–6; Fri 9–5, Apr–Oct; Sun–Thu 9–4.30, Fri 9–2, rest of year
- Staroměstská
- Few
- Moderate
- Uměleckoprůmyslové muzeum (Decorative Arts Museum, ► 39), Old Jewish Cemetery (► 42) Staroměstské náměstí (Old Town Square, ► 44)

Starý židovský hřbitov

HIGHLIGHTS

Around the cemetery

- Jewish Town Hall with Hebraic clock
- Klausen Synagogue (Jewish traditions exhibit)
- Ceremonial Hall
- Pinkas Synagogue (77,297 names of Holocaust victims; pictures from Terezín)
- Spanish Synagogue
- Maisel Synagogue (Jewish history exhibit)
- Statue of Rabbi Loew on Magistrát building, Mariánské náměstí

In the cemetery

- Tombstone of Rabbi Loew (c.1525–1609)
- Tombstone of Mayor Maisel (1528–1601)

INFORMATION

- ✛ E4: Locator map D2
- ✉ Cemetery: enter through the Pinkas Synagogue, Široká 3
- ☎ Prague Jewish Museum 224 819 456
- ⏲ Jewish Museum: Sun–Fri 9–6, Apr–Oct; 9–4.30, rest of year. Closed on Jewish holidays
- 🚇 Staroměstská
- ♿ Fair
- 💲 Expensive
- ↔ Staronová synagóga (► 41)
  Staroměstské náměstí (► 44)

Just as the sunlight filtering through the tall trees is reduced to a dappled shade, so visitors' voices diminish to a hush as they contemplate the 12,000 toppling tombstones of the Old Jewish Cemetery.

The changing Ghetto   Over the centuries, the Jewish Ghetto, hemmed in by its walls, became intolerably crowded. By the time Emperor Joseph II gave the Jews partial emancipation towards the end of the 18th century, the Ghetto had 12,000 inhabitants, crammed together within it in increasingly sordid conditions. During the course of the 19th century many moved out to more salubrious quarters in the suburbs. Around 1900, the city fathers decided to 'improve' the district, by then named Josefov ('Joseph's Town') in honour of the emperor. Most of it was flattened to make way for broad streets and boulevards, though the rococo Jewish Town Hall and a clutch of synagogues around the cemetery were spared. They survived under the German occupation, some say, because Hitler hoped to preserve what was left of the Ghetto as a 'Museum of a Vanished Race'. The stolen valuables of the Jewish communities of Bohemia and Moravia were brought to Prague, where some are now on display in the synagogues administered by the Prague Jewish Museum.

Solemn cemetery   The cemetery is evocative of the long centuries of Jewish life in Prague. Unable to extend it, the custodians were forced to bury the dead one on top of the other, up to 12 deep in places. The total number laid to rest here may amount to 80,000. Visitors leave wishful notes under pebbles on the more prominent tombstones (like that of Rabbi Loew, ► 41).

Anežský klášter

St. Agnes's Convent, the city's most venerable Gothic complex, shelters in a quiet precinct of the Old Town. Once earmarked for destruction, it is now the fitting home for one of the country's most distinctive galleries.

Canonized Czech Agnes was a 13th-century princess, sister of Wenceslas I and founder of a convent of Poor Clares here. In its glory days St. Agnes's was a mausoleum for the royal family, but was sacked by the Hussites in the 15th century. In 1782, it was closed down by Joseph II, and became slum housing until city authorities decided to raze it in the 1890s, only relenting when faced with bitter public protest. The convent was slowly restored, and, in November 1989, days before the Communist regime ended, Agnes was made a saint. An auspicious omen?

Bohemian Renaissance The convent now displays the National Gallery's collection of medieval art from Czech lands and nearby. The magnificent paintings and sculptures show the extraordinary achievements made by the fine arts in Bohemia, above all during the reigns of Emperor Charles IV and his successors. Prague's court artists fused Italian, French and Flemish influences in a manner all their own, pointing towards the late-Gothic style that flourished in Europe.

HIGHLIGHTS

- *Madonna of Vyšehrad* painting
- *Madonna and Child* sculpture from Český Krumlov
- Panel paintings by the Master of Vyšší Brod
- Portraits of saints by Master Theodoricus
- *Christ on the Mount of Olives* by the Třeboň Master
- Votive altarpiece from Zlichov
- *Madonna of Poleň,* Cranach the Elder
- Vaulted medieval cloister
- Church of St. Francis (concert hall)
- Church of the Holy Saviour

INFORMATION

- ✚ E3: Locator map D2
- ✉ U milosrdných 17, Staré Město
- ☎ 224 810 628
- 🕐 Tue–Sun 10–6
- Ⓜ Náměstí Republiky
- 🚊 Tram 17 (Právnická fakulta stop) or tram 5, 14 (Dlouhá třída stop)
- ♿ Fair
- 💷 Moderate

Musicians perform at St. Agnes's Convent

43

Staroměstské náměstí

HIGHLIGHTS

- Orloj (Astronomical Clock) from the 15th century (➤ 61)
- Council Hall and Clock Tower (➤ 53) of Old Town Hall
- Sgraffitoed House at the Minute dated 1611 (No. 2)
- Kostel sv Mikuláše (the baroque Church of St. Nicholas)
- Jan Hus Memorial of 1915
- Pavement crosses in front of Old Town Hall
- Palác Goltz-Kinských (➤ 54)
- The Gothic Dům u Kamenného Zvonu (House at the Stone Bell)
- Renaissance house (No 14)
- Arcaded houses Nos. 22–26, with baroque façades and medieval interiors and cellars

INFORMATION

- E4: Locator map D2
- Staroměstské náměstí, Staré Město
- Restaurants and cafés
- Staroměstská
- Fair
- Staronová synagóga, Josefov (➤ 41)

Visitors throng the spacious Old Town Square at all times of year, entertained by street performers, refreshed at outdoor cafés and enchanted by the Orloj —the Astronomical Clock—and the cheerful façades of the old buildings.

Square and Týn Church

Martyrs and mournful memories The Old Town Square has not always been so jolly. The medieval marketplace became a scene of execution where Hussites lost their heads in the 15th century and 27 prominent Protestants were put to death in 1621 (they are commemorated by white crosses in the pavement). In 1945, in a final act of spite, diehard Nazis demolished a whole wing of the Old Town Hall; the site has still not been built on. On 25 February 1948, Premier Gottwald proclaimed the triumph of Communism from the rococo Goltz-Kinský Palace.

Around the square The hub of the square is the Jan Hus Memorial, an extraordinary art-nouveau sculpture whose base is one of the few places in the square where you can sit without having to buy a drink. To your left rise the blackened towers of the Týn Church (➤ 57), while to your right is the Old Town Hall, an attractively varied assembly of buildings and, further around, the city's second St. Nicholas's Church. The fine town houses surrounding the square are a study in various architectural styles, from the genuine Gothic House at the Stone Bell to the 19th-century Gothic Revival No. 16.

Václavské náměstí

Despite its sometimes rather seedy air, Wenceslas Square is still the place where the city's heart beats most strongly, and to meet someone 'beneath the horse' (the Wenceslas statue) remains a special thrill.

When is a square not a square? When it's a boulevard. 'Václavák', 700m (2,300ft) long, slopes gently up to the imposing façade of the National Museum (➤ 46), which is fronted by the statue of Wenceslas on his sprightly steed. This is a good place to arrange a rendezvous—whatever the time of day there's always some action, with daytime shoppers and sightseers replaced by every species of night owl as darkness falls.

History in the making Many dramas of modern times have been played out in Wenceslas Square. The new state of Czechoslovakia was proclaimed here in 1918, and in 1939 German tanks underlined the republic's demise. In 1968, more tanks arrived—this time to crush the Prague Spring of Alexander Dubček. To protest at the Soviet occupation, Jan Palach burned himself to death here the following year, and in 1989 Dubček and Václav Havel waved from the balcony of No. 36 as half a million Czechs crowded the square to celebrate the collapse of Communism.

Museum of modern architecture The procession of buildings lining both sides of the square, from the resplendent art-nouveau Hotel Evropa (➤ 71) to the elegant Functionalist Baťa Store, tells the story of the distinctively Czech contribution to 20th-century architecture and design. Even more intriguing are the arcades (*pasáž*) that burrow deep into the buildings, creating a labyrinthine world of boutiques, theatres, cafés and cinemas.

HIGHLIGHTS

- *St. Wenceslas* statue, Josef Myslbek (1912)
- Arcades of the Lucerna Palace
- Hotel Evropa, completed 1905 (No. 25)
- 1920s Functionalist Baťa and Lindt buildings (Nos. 4, 6,)
- Ambassador, late art-nouveau hotel of 1912 (No. 5)
- Memorial to the victims of Communism
- 1950s Soviet-style Jalta Hotel (No. 45)
- Former Bank of Moravia of 1916 (Nos. 38–40)
- Art-nouveau Peterka building of 1900 (No. 12)
- Koruna Palace of 1914 (No. 1)

INFORMATION

- ✚ E4–E5: Locator map D2
- ✉ Václavské náměstí, Nové Město
- 🍴 Many restaurants and cafés
- 🚇 Můstek or Muzeum
- ♿ Fair
- ↔ Národní muzeum (National Museum ➤ 46)

Národní muzeum

HIGHLIGHTS

- Allegorical sculptures on the terrace
- The Pantheon and dome
- Coin collection
- Collection of precious stones
- Skeleton of a whale

INFORMATION

- F5: Locator map E3
- Václavské náměstí 68, Nové Mèsto
- 224 497 111
- Daily 9–5, Oct–Apr; 10–6, rest of year. Closed first Tue of month
- Café
- Muzeum
- Few
- Moderate
- Václavské náměstí (Wenceslas Square, ➤ 45)

Some people find Prague's National Museum disappointing, crammed as it is with cabinets full of beetles and mineral specimens. However, try to enjoy it as a period piece in its own right, for its dusty showcases are as venerable as the building itself.

Top building   With its gilded dome crowning the rise at the top of Václavské náměstí (Wenceslas Square, ➤ 45), Prague's National Museum provides a grand finale to the capital's most important street. The neo-Renaissance building was completed in 1891, and at the time was as much an object of pride to the Czech populace as the Národní divadlo (National Theatre ➤ 38). Such is its presence that some visitors have mistaken it for the parliament building, as did the Soviet gunner who raked its façade with machine-gun fire in August 1968.

An array of -ologies   Even if you are not a keen entomologist, paleontologist, zoologist, mineralogist or numismatist, you can't fail to be impressed by the evidence assembled here of the 19th century's great passion for collecting and classifying. Perhaps more immediately attractive are the temporary exhibitions, which draw on the museum's vast collections; the dinosaur display is likely to prove compelling to young

Allegorical figure of the River Vltava, on the stairway leading up to the National Museum

visitors. Above all, the building itself is impressive, with its grand stairways, statuary, mosaics and patterned floors. And unlike most other attractions in Prague, it's open on Mondays.

Národní technické muzeum

Did you know that Czechoslovakia had one of the world's biggest auto industries and that Škoda cars are legendary for their reliability? That a horse-drawn railway once linked Bohemia with Austria? That a Czechoslovak fleet once sailed the oceans?

Past glories The answer to all these questions will be 'yes', after you've visited the wonderful National Technical Museum, off the beaten track on the edge of Letenské sady (Letná Plain). The facelessness of the building belies the richness and fascination of its contents, a celebration of the longstanding technological prowess of inventive and hard-working Czechs. The Czech provinces were the industrial power-house of the Austro-Hungarian Empire, their steel works and coal mines providing the foundation for excellence in engineering of all kinds, from the production of weapons to locomotive manufacture. Later, between the two world wars, independent Czechoslovakia's light industries led the world in innovativeness and quality.

Trains and boats and planes The museum's collection of technological artefacts is displayed to spectacular effect in the vast glass-roofed and galleried main hall, where balloons and biplanes hang in space above ranks of sinister-looking streamlined limousines and powerful steam engines. The side galleries tell the story of 'The Wheel' and of navigation, from rafting timber on the Vltava to transporting ore across the oceans in the Czechoslovak carrier *Košice*. Deep underground there's a mock-up of a coal mine, and other sections tell you all you ever wanted to know about time, sound, geodesy, photography and astronomy.

HIGHLIGHTS

- 1928 Škoda fire engine
- Laurin and Klement soft-top roadster
- President Masaryk's V-12 Tatra
- Soviet ZIS 110B limousine
- Express locomotive 375-007 of 1911
- Imperial family's railway dining car of 1891
- Bleriot XI Kašpar monoplane
- Sokol monoplane

INFORMATION

- E3: Locator map D1
- Kostelní 42, Holešovice
- 220 399 111
- Tue–Sun 9–5
- Trams 1, 8, 18, 26 to Letenské náměstí, or Metro Vltavská then tram 1 to Letenské náměstí
- Few
- Moderate
- Veletržní palác (Museum of Modern Art, ► 49), Letenské sady (Letná Plain, ► 52)

Obecní dům

The prosaic name 'Municipal House' fails utterly to convey anything of the character of this extraordinary art-nouveau building, a gloriously extravagant early 20th-century confection on which every artist of the day seems to have left his stamp.

City council citadel Glittering like some gigantic, flamboyant jewel, more brightly than ever since its 1997 restoration, the Obecní dům is linked to the blackened Prašná brána (Powder Tower, ➤ 52), last relic of the Old Town's fortifications and long one of the city's main symbols. The intention of the city fathers in the first years of the 20th century was to add an even more powerful element to the cityscape that would celebrate the glory of the Czech nation and Prague's place within it. The site of the old Royal Palace was selected, and no expense was spared to erect a megastructure in which the city's burgeoning life could expand.

Ornamental orgy The building programme included meeting and assembly rooms, cafés, restaurants, bars, even a pâtisserie, while the mayor was provided with particularly luxurious quarters. The 1,149-seat Smetana Hall, home of the Prague Symphony Orchestra, is a temple to the muse of Bohemian music. Everything is encrusted with lavish decoration, in stucco, glass, mosaic, murals, metalwork and textiles.

The glittering portal of the Obecní dům

Veletržní palác

'A truly great experience was a tour of the Prague Trade Fair Building. The first impression... is breathtaking.' So enthused the architect Le Corbusier in 1928, shortly after this monumental structure, now the Museum of Modern Art, was completed.

Trailblazer Never lacking in ego, the great master builder and design pioneer Le Corbusier was none the less vexed to find that his Czech colleagues had got in first in completing what is one of the key buildings in the evolution of 20th-century design, a secular, modern-day cathedral constructed in concrete, steel and glass. Set in the suburb of Holešovice, the palace was intended to be a showpiece for the products of Czechoslovakia. However, trade fairs moved away from Prague to Brno, and for many years the great building languished in neglect and obscurity, its originality forgotten as its architectural innovations became the norm throughout the world.

Disguised blessing After fire gutted the palace in 1974, it was decided to use its elegant spaces to display the National Gallery's modern art treasures, which had previously been hidden away without a proper home. In all, it took around 20 years to complete the restoration work. Now the engrossing Czech 19th-century collection leads the way to the amazing achievements of Czech painters and sculptors in the early part of the 20th century. The museum also shows works by the French Impressionists and other modern foreign paintings, and promotes contemporary arts of all types, staging the kind of major international art shows of which the Czechs were so long deprived.

HIGHLIGHTS

- *Winter Evening in Town*, Jakub Schikaneder
- *Reader of Dostoyevsky*, Emil Filla
- *Serie C VI*, František Kupka
- *Melancholy*, Jan Zrzavý
- *Sailor*, Karel Dvořák
- *Self-portrait*, Picasso
- *Self-portrait*, Douanier Rousseau
- *Green Rye*, Van Gogh
- *Virgin*, Gustav Klimt
- *Pregnant Woman and Death*, Egon Schiele

INFORMATION

- ✛ F2: Locator map E1
- ✉ Dukelských hrdinů 47, Holešovice
- ☎ 224 301 111
- 🕐 Tue–Wed, Fri–Sun 10–6, Thu 10–9
- 🍴 Café
- Ⓜ Vltavská
- 🚊 Tram 5 from Náměstí Republiky
- ♿ Good
- 💲 Moderate
- ↔ Národní technické muzeum (National Technical Museum ➤ 47)

Top: Green Rye, *by Van Gogh*

Trojský zámek

Out here you catch a glimpse of how delightful Prague's countryside must have been three centuries ago, with vine-clad slopes, trees in abundance and the resplendent Troja Château among the allées and parterres.

Prague's Versailles This extravagant baroque palace was built not by the monarch, but by the second richest man in Prague, Count Wenceslas Adelbert Šternberg. The Šternbergs profited from the Thirty Years War, and at the end of the 17th century were in a position to commission Jean-Baptiste Mathey to design a country house along the lines of the contemporary châteaux of the architect's native France. The south-facing site by the river, orientated directly on St. Vitus's Cathedral and Prague Castle on the far side of the Royal Hunting Grounds, now Stromovka Park, was ideal for Šternberg, allowing him to offer the monarch the right kind of hospitality following a day's hunting.

Ornamental extravagance The palace's proportions are grandiose, and its painted interiors go over the top in paying homage to the country's Habsburg rulers. And over the top, too, goes a turbaned Turk as he topples, in stunning trompe l'oeil, from the mock battlements in the grand hall. Troja was acquired by the state in the 1920s, but restored only in the late 1980s (some think excessively). It contains part of Prague's collection of 19th-century paintings, few of which can compete with the flamboyance of their setting.

Troja's grounds abound in ornamentation

PRAGUE's
best

51

Panoramas

ACROSS THE RIVER

Some of the finest views of
Prague are those in which the
city is seen across the broad
waters of the Vltava, as from
the Smetana statue or Kampa
Island. A stroll along the
embankments and footpaths
on both sides of the river is
equally rewarding, as are the
islands–Slovanský ostrov
(Slavonic Island) and Střelecký
ostrov (Shooters' Island).

EMBANKMENT, KAMPA ISLAND

From the shady parkland of Kampa Island there is an
unusual view across the Vltava over Karlův most
(Charles Bridge) and the weir to the Old Town.
🛑 D4 ☒ U Sovových mlýnů ③ Permanently open 🚊 Trams 12,
22, 23 to Hellichova 🐾 Free

KATEDRÁLA SV VÍTA
(TOWER, ST. VITUS'S CATHEDRAL)

Climb the 287 steps of St. Vitus's Cathedral tower for
one of the best panoramas of the city and close-ups
of the cathedral (► 32), with its bristling buttresses,
diamond-tiled roofs and copper cockerels.
🛑 C/D4 ☒ Pražský hrad ③ Daily 10–5, Apr–Oct 🍽 Cafés and
restaurants 🚊 Trams 22, 23 to Pražský hrad 🐾 Inexpensive

LETENSKÉ SADY (LETNÁ PLAIN)

These parks and gardens stretch from the eastern
end of Prague Castle (► 31), high above the banks of
the Vltava. Between 1955 and 1962 a monster statue
of Stalin stood here. The plinth, now infested with
skateboarders, is occupied by a giant metronome,
and makes an excellent vantage point over the river.
🛑 D–E3 ☒ Letenské sady ③ Always accessible 🚇 Malostranská
and uphill walk 🚊 Tram 18 to Chotkovy sady or 22, 23 to Královský
letohrádek 🐾 Free

Malá Strana from Petřín

PRAŠNÁ BRÁNA (POWDER TOWER)

The sumptuous roofscape of the adjoining Obecní dům (Municipal House, ► 48)
makes an immediate impact, but this
panorama is particularly appealing
because of the vista along Celetná Street
into the heart of the Old Town.
🛑 E/F4 ☒ Náměstí Republiky ③ Daily 10–6,
Mar–Oct 🚇 Náměstí Republiky 🚊 Trams 5, 14 to
Náměstí Republiky 🐾 Inexpensive

ROZHLEDNA
(PETŘÍN HILL LOOKOUT TOWER)

This little brother of the Eiffel Tower was
erected for Prague's great Jubilee Expo of
1891. Prepare to climb 299 steps.
🛑 C4 ☒ Petřín ③ Daily 10–7, Apr–Aug; 10–6,
Sep–Oct; Sat–Sun 10–5, rest of year 🚊 Tram 12, 22,
23 to Hellichova, then Lanovka funicular (from Újezd)
🐾 Inexpensive

SMETANA STATUE

The walkway leading to the Muzeum
Bedřicha Smetany (the Smetana
Museum, ► 59) is in fact a pier (known as
Novotného lávka), built out into the river.
At its very tip are café tables and a statue

of the composer; the view across the river, whose roaring weir drowns all intrusive noises, is the classic one of Charles Bridge, Malá Strana and Prague Castle above.

✚ D4 ✉ Novotného lávka 🕐 Always open 🍴 Café and restaurant Ⓜ Staroměstská 🚊 Trams 17, 18 to Karlovy lázně 💰 Free

STAROMĚSTSKÁ RADNICE (TOWER, OLD TOWN HALL)

The climb, on foot or by lift, up the tower of the Old Town Hall is well worth while for the dizzying view it gives of the swarming activity in Old Town Square (▶ 44), as well as of the higgledy-piggledy red-tiled roofs of the medieval Old Town.

✚ E4 ✉ Staroměstské náměsti 🕐 Tue–Sun 9–6, Mon 11–6, Apr–Sep; Tue–Sun 9–5, Mon 11–5, rest of year 🍴 Restaurants in square Ⓜ Staroměstská 💰 Moderate

STARÝ KRÁLOVSKÝ PALÁC (OLD ROYAL PALACE)

After admiring the interiors of the Old Royal Palace and the Vladislav Hall, take a stroll on the south-facing terrace or peep through the windows from which the Catholic councillors were thrown out in 1618. All Prague lies at your feet.

✚ D4 ✉ Pražský hrad ☎ 224 373 368 🕐 Daily 9–5, Apr–Oct; 9–4, rest of year 🍴 Cafés and restaurants 🚊 Tram 22, 23 to Pražský hrad 💰 Moderate

TELEVIZNÍ VYSÍLAČ (TELEVISION TOWER)

This immense television transmitter tower in the inner suburb of Žižkov, 216m (710ft) tall, may be a blot on Prague's townscape, but its gallery does give visitors stupendous views over the city and its surroundings. The best time to take the lift to the top is fairly early in the day, before the sun has moved too far around to the west.

✚ G5 ✉ Mahlerovy sady ☎ 267 005 784 🕐 Daily 10am–11pm 🍴 Restaurant Ⓜ Jiřího z Poděbrad 🚊 Trams 5, 9, 26 to Lipanská 💰 Moderate

VYŠEHRAD

A walk around the ramparts of the old fortifications of Vyšehrad gives contrasting views along the Vltava far below. Upstream, Prague is surprisingly countrified, with rough woodland and rugged lime-stone crags, while downstream the panorama reveals the city, especially Hradčany, from an entirely new angle. Nearby, the terraces of the Communists' huge Palace of Culture (now the Congress Centre) offer a view across the deep Nusle ravine towards the New Town, guarded by the walls of the Karlov Monastery.

✚ E6/7 ✉ Vyšehrad 🕐 Permanently accessible 🍴 Restaurant Ⓜ Vyšehrad 🚊 Trams 3, 7, 17 to Výtoň

Old Town Square from the Old Town Hall tower

UNPOPULAR NEIGHBOUR

Building the unlovely TV tower in Žižkov necessitated destroying part of an old Jewish cemetery and was resisted by locals and other protesters (in so far as any resistance was possible in Communist days). Some people are still uneasy, claiming that they pick up transmissions on virtually any metal object, or that their bodies are being slowly microwaved.

Galleries

UNSEEN ART

Housing Prague's vast and varied art collections has always posed problems. Under Communism, many pictures and other art objects were kept more or less permanently in storage, and the unique Czech contribution to 20th-century art was never properly celebrated. The big issue is now a financial one. If there are particular works you want to see, check whether they are actually on display before you make a detour to see them.

DŮM U ZLATÉHO PRSTENU (HOUSE AT THE GOLDEN RING)

The Prague City Gallery's fine collection of 20th- and 21st-century Czech art. The gallery stages large exhibitions a few steps away at the House at the Stone Bell, a Gothic tower house that restorers discovered behind a rococo façade in the 1960s.

✚ E4 ✉ Týnská 6, Staré Město ☎ 224 827 022 ⏰ Tue–Sun 10–6 🍴 Cafés and restaurants 🚇 Staroměstská 🖐 Moderate

LAPIDÁRIUM

Masterpieces of Czech sculpture, including some of the original statues from Karlův most (Charles Bridge, ➤ 37), brought here for protection.

✚ F2 ✉ Výstaviště, Holešovice ☎ 233 375 636 ⏰ Tue–Fri noon–6, Sat–Sun 10–6 🍴 Restaurants and cafés in grounds 🚇 Nádraži Holešovice 🚊 Trams 5, 12, 17 to Výstaviště 🖐 Inexpensive

PALÁC GOLTZ-KINSKÝCH (GOLTZ-KINSKÝ PALACE)

The National Gallery's flagship space for changing exhibitions of all kinds. It was from a balcony here that Klement Gottwald proclaimed the victory of the working classes in 1948.

✚ E4 ✉ Staroměstské náměstí 12 ☎ 224 810 758 ⏰ Tue–Sun 10–6 🍴 Cafés and restaurants in Old Town Square 🚇 Staroměstská 🖐 Moderate

House at the Stone Bell

OBRAZÁRNA (PRAGUE CASTLE PICTURE GALLERY)

Mannerist and baroque paintings and sculptures, handsomely displayed, recall the fervent creative atmosphere at the castle under Rudolph II.

✚ C4 ✉ Second Courtyard, Prague Castle, Hradčany ☎ 224 373 368 ⏰ Daily 10–6 🍴 Cafés and restaurants in castle 🚊 Trams 22, 23 to Pražský hrad 🖐 Moderate

Museums

BERTRAMKA (MOZART MUSEUM)

Mozart's closest friends in Prague were the Dušeks, and the Bertramka was their rural retreat. This is the place where the great composer dashed off the last lines of *Don Giovanni* before conducting its premiere in the Stavovské divadlo (Estates Theatre, ➤ 77).
➕ C6 ✉ Mozartova 169, Smíchov ☎ 257 318 461 🕐 Daily 9.30–6, Apr–Oct; 9.30–5, rest of year 🚇 Anděl, then Tram 4, 7, 9, 10 to Bertramka (one stop) 🎫 Inexpensive

MUZEUM HLAVNÍHO MĚSTA PRAHY (CITY MUSEUM)

This pompous late 19th-century building contains exhibits telling the story of Prague's evolution from the earliest times. The star is a scale model of the city as it was in the 1820s and 1830s, meticulously put together by a person of infinite patience named Antonín Langweil. Most of the extensive collections are in storage, but selections are shown in rotation.
➕ F4 ✉ Na poříčí 52, north Nové Město ☎ 224 816 772 🕐 Tue–Sun 9–6 🚇 Florenc 🎫 Inexpensive

MUZEUM POLICIE ČR (POLICE MUSEUM)

This museum recovered quickly from the collapse of the old order in 1989 and gives an upbeat account of Czech policing, with plenty of gore and weaponry on show in, incongruously, what was once the Karlov Monastery.
➕ E6 ✉ Ke Karlovu 1, Nové Město ☎ 224 923 619 🕐 Tue–Sun 10–5 🚇 I P Pavlova or Vyšehrad 🎫 Inexpensive

NÁPRSTKOVO MUZEUM (NÁPRSTEK MUSEUM)

Intriguing ethnographical exhibits assembled by a 19th-century collector in love with the indigenous cultures of the Americas, Africa and the Pacific.
➕ E4 ✉ Betlémské náměstí 1, Staré Město ☎ 224 497 500 🕐 Tue–Sun 9–noon, 12.45–5.30 🚇 Staroměstská or Národní třída 🎫 Inexpensive

SBÍRKA MIMOEVROPSKÉHO UMĚNÍ (ASIAN ART MUSEUM)

A magnificent baroque chateau houses the National Gallery's extensive Chinese and Japanese collections and smaller displays of Islamic and South Asian art. It's one hour from the city centre by metro and bus.
➕ Off map, 13km south of the centre ✉ Zámek Zbraslav, Zbraslav ☎ 257 921 638 🕐 Tue–Sun 10–6 🚇 Smíchovské nádraží, then bus 129, 241, 243, 255, 360 to Zbraslavské náměstí 🎫 Moderate

THE BIG GUNS

Czech and Slovak involvement in the big conflict that never happened, the face-off of the Cold War, is chillingly displayed in the huge collection of military hardware on show at the Letecké muzeum (Aircraft Museum) at Kbely airfield, on the city's eastern outskirts. Some of the aircraft date back to World War I, but above all it's the Russian MiG jetfighters that remain in the memory.

MORE MILITARIA

Almost unknown abroad, the tale of Czech and Slovak involvement in the conflicts of the 20th century is told in the Armádní muzeum (Army Museum) at the foot of the National Memorial in the inner suburb of Žižkov.

Palaces

AUTO SCULPTURE

In summer 1989, the streets around the West German Embassy were clogged with Wartburgs and Trabants abandoned by their East German owners. A fibreglass Trabant on mighty legs now stands in the embassy garden as a memorial to those days.

Coat of arms, Archbishop's Palace

HIGH DIPLOMACY

The Anglophile and athletic first president of Czechoslovakia, Tomáš Garringue Masaryk, is said to have maintained good relations with the British ambassador in the Thun Palace, on Malá Strana's tiny Thunovská street, by climbing down a ladder set against Prague Castle's walls to drop in for tea.

ARCIBISKUPSKÝ PALÁC (ARCHBISHOP'S PALACE)

The lusciously restored rococo façade hides a sumptuous residence, unfortunately accessible only on special occasions.

➕ C4 ✉ Hradčanské náměstí 16, Hradčany ⓒ Not normally open to the public 🚊 Trams 22, 23 to Pražský hrad

ČERNÍNSKÝ PALÁC (ČERNÍN PALACE)

It was from this huge baroque structure (completed 1720), now the Foreign Ministry, that Jan Masaryk fell to his death in 1948.

➕ C4 ✉ Loretánské náměstí, Hradčany ⓒ Not open to the public 🚊 Tram 22, 23 to Pohořelec

DŮM PÁNŮ Z KUNŠTÁTU A PODĚBRAD (HOUSE OF THE LORDS OF KUNŠTÁT AND PODĚBRADY)

This Romanesque-Gothic mansion is possibly the most ancient interior accessible to the public. It was home to King George of Poděbrady in the 15th century.

➕ E4 ✉ Řetězová 3, Staré Město ⓒ Tue–Sun 10–6, May–Sep 🚇 Staroměstská 🎟 Inexpensive

LOBKOVICKÝ PALÁC (LOBKOVIC PALACE)

This superb baroque structure (not to be confused with the Lobkovic Palace within the castle precinct), the residence of the German ambassador, saw strange scenes in summer 1989, when it became a temporary home to thousands of East Germans seeking refuge.

➕ C4 ✉ Vlašská 19, Malá Strana ⓒ Not open to the public 🚊 Tram 12, 22, 23 to Malostranské náměstí

SCHÖNBORNSKÝ PALÁC (SCHÖNBORN-COLLOREDO PALACE)

The US Embassy occupies a baroque palace whose grandeur equals that of the nearby German Embassy.

➕ D4 ✉ Tržiště 15, Malá Strana ⓒ Not open to the public 🚊 Tram 12, 22, 23 to Malostranské náměstí

SCHWARZENBERSKÝ PALÁC (SCHWARZENBERG PALACE)

The city's most imposing Renaissance palace sits just outside Prague Castle, its sgraffito-bedecked façade and bristling gables making a noble impression. The palace houses a museum of military history.

➕ C4 ✉ Hradčanské náměstí 2, Hradčany ☎ 222 202 398 ⓒ Closed for reconstruction 🚊 Trams 22, 23 to Pražský hrad

Churches

In the Top 25

BETLÉMSKÁ KAPLE (BETHLEHEM CHAPEL)

You must see this barn-like structure where Jan Hus preached to really appreciate the deeply nonconformist traditions so thoroughly obscured by centuries of imposed Catholicism. The chapel, in the Old Town, was totally reconstructed in the 1950s.
🚼 E4 ⊠ Betlémské náměstí, Staré Město 🕒 Tue–Sun 10–6.30, Apr–Oct; 10–5.30, rest of year 🍴 Restaurants and cafés nearby 🚇 Národní třída 🎫 Inexpensive

KOSTEL PANNY MARIE PŘED TÝNEM (TÝN CHURCH)

Among the city's best-known landmarks is the Gothic Týn Church, whose twin towers stick up spikily behind the houses east of Old Town Square. Inside are some fascinating tombs.
🚼 E4 ⊠ Týnská and Celetná, Staré Město 🕒 May be open only for services due to reconstruction 🍴 Cafés and restaurants nearby 🚇 Staroměstská or Náměstí Republiky

KOSTEL PANNY MARIE VÍTĚZNÉ (CHURCH OF OUR LADY VICTORIOUS)

After Czech Protestantism was crushed in 1621, this church became a centre of the Counter-Reformation, thanks not least to miracles wrought by the Bambino di Praga waxwork (see panel).
🚼 D4 ⊠ Karmelitská 9, Malá Strana 🕒 Mon–Sat 8.30–5.30, Sun 1–5 🚋 Tram 12, 22, 23 to Hellichova

KOSTEL SV JAKUBA (ST. JAMES'S CHURCH)

Beneath the baroque froth is an ancient Gothic church, though you'd hardly guess it. The acoustics of the long nave are particularly impressive, and concerts held here are generally well attended.
🚼 E4 ⊠ Malá Štupartská, Staré Město 🕒 Daily 9.30–4 🚇 Náměstí Republiky

KOSTEL SV MIKULÁŠE, STARÉ MĚSTO (ST. NICHOLAS'S CHURCH, OLD TOWN)

St. Nicholas's twin towers and grand dome are the work of the great baroque architect Kilian Ignaz Dientzenhofer. His church is now a prominent feature of Old Town Square, but it was originally designed to fit the narrow street that once ran there.
🚼 E4 ⊠ Staroměstské náměstí, Staré Město 🕒 Tue–Sat 10–4, Mon noon–4, Sun noon–3, Apr–Oct; Tue, Thu, Fri, Sun 10–noon, Wed 10–4, rest of year 🚇 Staroměstská

Týn Church

ROUGH JUSTICE

A withered hand hangs from the wall to the right of the entrance in St. James's Church, severed by a butcher when the thief to whom it belonged was apprehended by a statue of the Virgin Mary, who refused to let go.

BAMBINO DI PRAGA

The Bambino di Praga waxwork, known here as the Pražské Jezulátko, was given to the Church of Our Lady Victorious in 1628 as part of the re-Catholicization imposed on the wayward Czechs. The miracles performed by the diminutive effigy of the infant Jesus are even more numerous than its 60 sumptuous changes of outfit.

Twentieth-Century Buildings

ART NOUVEAU

The glorious effusions of art nouveau, with its use of sinuous lines and motifs from the natural world, mark the townscape all over the city. Prague rivals Vienna in the number of edifices built in this style, known here as Secession.

The famous Black Madonna

CZECH INNOVATIONS

Art nouveau/Secession was an international style, but later Czech architects created unique movements of their own—cubist architecture, for instance, and the intricate Rondo-Cubism that then followed.

BANKA LEGIÍ (BANK OF THE LEGIONS)

Czechoslovak legionaries fought on many fronts in World War I, and the sculptures decorating the façade of this handsome Rondo-Cubist (see panel) building of 1923 commemorate their exploits.

➕ F4 ✉ Na poříčí 24, north Nové Město 🕐 Accessible during banking hours 🚇 Náměstí Republiky

CUBIST STREET LAMP

This extraordinary little object, an echo of Czech Cubism, still seems to vibrate with the artistic excitements that suffused metropolitan life in early 20th-century Prague.

➕ E5 ✉ Jungmannovo náměstí, Nové Město 🚇 Můstek

DŮM U ČERNÉ MATKY BOŽÍ (HOUSE AT THE BLACK MADONNA)

This striking example of Czech Cubist architecture, designed by Josef Gočár (1912), stands challengingly at the corner of Celetná Street in the heart of the Old Town, yet somehow manages to harmonize with its surroundings. Look for the Black Madonna in her gilded cage.

➕ E4 ✉ Ovocný trh 19, Staré Město 🚇 Náměstí Republiky

HLAVNÍ NÁDRAŽÍ (MAIN STATION)

Above the modern concourses rise the richly ornamented art-nouveau buildings of Prague's main station (1909), originally named after Emperor Franz Joseph, then after President Wilson.

➕ F4 ✉ Wilsonova 1, Nové Město 🕐 24 hours 🍴 Buffet, café 🚇 Hlavní nádraží 🎫 Free

KOSTEL U NEJSVĚTĚJŠÍHO SRDCE PAUÉ (CHURCH OF THE MOST SACRED HEART OF OUR LORD)

Looking like a cross between a Roman basilica and a train station, this is Slovenian architect Joze Plečnik's most stunning Prague work. Finished in 1932, it dominates not just the square but the whole neighbourhood.

➕ G5 ✉ Náměstí Jiřiho z Poděbrad 🚇 Jiřiho z Poděbrad

NOS. 7 & 9 NÁRODNÍ (NÁRODNÍ TŘÍDA)

Fascinating variations on the theme of art nouveau can be traced in the façades of these adjoining office buildings. Both were designed by Osvald Polívka; No. 9 was built for the publisher Topič and No. 7 for an insurance company.

➕ E5 ✉ Národní 7 & 9, Nové Město 🚇 Národní třída

For Music Lovers

BERTRAMKA (MOZART MUSEUM, ► 55)

DVOŘÁK'S BIRTHPLACE

Dvořák was born the son of an innkeeper in the unassuming little village of Nelahozeves on the Elbe River. His birthplace, at the foot of the Lobkovic family's huge Renaissance castle, is now a museum.
➕ Off map, 32km (20 miles) northwest of Prague ✉ Nelahozeves 12
☎ 315 785 099 🕐 2nd, 3rd and 4th weekend 10–noon, 1–5, Apr–Oct; 2nd and 4th weekend 9–noon, 1–4, rest of year
🚉 Nelahozeves–zámek (one stop after Kralupy nad Vltavou)
💷 Inexpensive

MUZEUM BEDŘICHA SMETANY (SMETANA MUSEUM)

The museum dedicated to the composer of 'Vltava' is appropriately sited in a building that rises directly out of the river.
➕ D4 ✉ Novotného lávka 1, Staré Město ☎ 222 220 082
🕐 Wed–Mon 10–5 🚇 Staroměstská 💷 Inexpensive

RUDOLFINUM

Classical music lovers revere this elegant hall (► 78). Contemporary art buffs will find major exhibitions in the equally beautiful gallery, behind the auditorium.
➕ E4 ✉ Náměstí Jana Palacha, Staré město ☎ 227 059 352
🕐 Gallery Tue–Sun 10–6 🚇 Staroměstská

SMETANOVA SÍŇ (SMETANA HALL)

The highly decorated 1,149-seat Smetana Hall is the grandest space in the Obecní dům (Municipal House, ► 48). The Prague Spring music festival is heralded here every year with a rousing rendition of the symphonic poem *Má Vlast* (*My Country*).
➕ E/F4 ✉ Obecní dům, Náměstí Republiky ☎ 222 002 100
🕐 Check locally 🍴 Café and restaurant 🚇 Náměstí Republiky

STÁTNÍ OPERA PRAHA (STATE OPERA, ► 77)

STAVOVSKÉ DIVADLO (ESTATES THEATRE, ► 77)

VILA AMERIKA (DVOŘÁK MUSEUM)

This exquisite little villa was built for Count Michna in 1720 as a summer retreat, when this part of the New Town was still countryside. It now serves as a fascinating repository for Dvořák memorabilia (► 78).
➕ E6 ✉ Ke Karlovu 20, Nové Město ☎ 224 918 013
🕐 Tue–Sun 10–5 🚇 I P Pavlova 💷 Inexpensive

A MUSICAL NATION

Co Čech–to muzikant! ('All Czechs are musicians!') goes the saying, and this is certainly one of the most musical of nations. In the 18th century Bohemia supplied musicians and composers to the whole of Europe.

THE BEAT GOES ON

Fuelled by Radio Luxembourg and smuggled records, Czech rock 'n' roll attracted real rebels–the early fans of this 'Bigbeat' sound risked jail merely for throwing an unauthorized sockhop. The Popmuseum, a new attraction on Besední street, in Malá Strana, revives the 'Bigbeat' scene.

Dvořák's piano, Vila Amerika

59

Green Spaces

MONKISH RETREAT

The old garden of the Franciscan monks between Václavské náměstí (Wenceslas Square) and Jungmannovo náměstí (Jungmann Square) is a welcome oasis in the heart of the city.

BAROQUE GARDENS BELOW PRAŽSKÝ HRAD

The aristocrats in their palaces in Malá Strana at the foot of Prague Castle turned their interconnecting gardens into a paradise of arbours, gazebos, fountains and stairways. Now reopened after restoration, they can also be enjoyed from the castle's Ramparts Garden above.

➕ D4 ✉ Valdštejnská 10–14 and Valdštejnské náměstí 3, Malá Strana 🕓 Daily 10–6, Apr–Oct 🚇 Malostranská 🎫 Moderate

KAMPA ISLAND

Kampa Island was flooded regularly until the Vltava was tamed in the 1950s, discouraging building and leaving large parts of it undeveloped.

➕ D4–5 🕓 At all times 🚃 Tram 12, 22, 23 to Hellichova or Malostranské náměstí 🎫 Free

KRÁLOVSKÁ ZAHRADA (ROYAL GARDENS)

Fine old trees and formal gardens make a superb setting for several pleasure pavilions north of Prague Castle: the Baroque Riding School, the sgraffitoed Ball-Game Hall and the beautiful Belvedere.

➕ C/D3 ✉ Královská zahrada, Hradčany 🕓 Daily 10–6, Apr–Oct 🚃 Tram 22, 23 to Královský letohrádek or Pražský hrad 🎫 Free

LETENSKÉ SADY (LETNÁ PLAIN, ► 52)

VOJANOVY SADY (VOJAN GARDENS)

A peaceful retreat hidden away in Malá Strana.

➕ D4 ✉ U lužického semináře 17, Malá Strana 🕓 Daily 8–7 summer; daily 8–5 winter 🚇 Malostranská 🎫 Free

Stromovka Park, Holešovice

KARLOVO NÁMĚSTÍ

Karlovo náměstí (Charles Square) is more of a park than a square, and is a useful resting place when pounding the pavements becomes too tiring in this spread-out part of town.

VRTBOVSKÁ ZAHRADA (VRTBA GARDEN)

Prague's finest individual baroque garden has a splendid staircase, sculptures and a view over Malá Strana.

➕ D4 ✉ Karmelitská 25, Malá Strana 🕓 Daily 10–6, Apr–Oct 🚃 Tram 12, 22, 23 to Malostranské náměstí 🎫 Inexpensive

ZAHRADA NA VALECH (RAMPARTS GARDEN)

The gardens just to the south of Prague Castle were redesigned in the 1920s and embellished with sculptural objects, including a miniature pyramid.

➕ C–D4 ✉ Pražský hrad (Prague Castle), Hradčany 🕓 Daily 10–6, Apr–Oct 🚇 Malostranská then uphill walk 🚃 Tram 22, 23 to Pražský hrad 🎫 Free

For Children

In the Top 25

▨ **NÁRODNÍ TECHNICKÉ MUZEUM (► 47)**
🖪 **PETŘÍN HILL, WITH THE FUNICULAR,
VIEWING TOWER, HALL OF MIRRORS,
OBSERVATORY (► 30)**

CHANGING OF THE GUARD, PRAŽSKÝ HRAD

The blue-uniformed Castle Guard is ceremonially
relieved every day at noon at the western gate of
Prague Castle, with extra pomp on Sundays.

🞢 C4 ⊠ Pražský hrad, Hradčany 🕙 Daily at noon 🚊 Tram 22,
23 to Pražský hrad 🎟 Free

HISTORIC TRAM RIDE

A vintage tram trundles round a circuit linking the
city centre, Malá Strana and the Exhibition Grounds.

ORLOJ (ASTRONOMICAL CLOCK)

Crowds gather every hour on the hour in front of the
Old Town Hall to enjoy the performance put on by
this fascinating clock, which not only tells the time
but gives the position of the sun, moon and much
more, while the splendid painted calendar shows
saints' days, the signs of the zodiac and the labours
of the months. Legend has it that Hanuš, the master
technician who perfected the mechanism, was
blinded by the city fathers to stop him passing his
secrets on. But Hanuš persuaded an apprentice to
lead him up inside the clock. He then plunged his
hands into the mechanism, putting it out of action
for 80 years.

🞢 E4 ⊠ Staroměstské náměstí 🕙 Performances daily on the hour
9–9 🚇 Staroměstská 🎟 Free

PUPPET THEATRES (► 82)

HORSE DRAWN CARRIAGES

Based in Old Town Square.

VÝSTAVIŠTĚ (EXHIBITION GROUNDS)

The extensive Exhibition Grounds in the inner
suburb of Holešovice have old-fashioned rides
among other attractions.

🞢 E–F2 ⊠ U Výstaviště, Holešovice ☎ 220103 204 🕙 Tue–Fri
from 2pm, Sat–Sun from 10am (evening opening for performances)
🍴 Cafés and restaurants 🚊 Tram 5, 12, 17 to Výstaviště
🎟 Inexpensive

ZOOLOGICKÁ ZAHRADA (ZOO)

Not world-class, but useful to know about and
conveniently placed opposite Troja Château (► 50).

🞢 D1 ⊠ U Trojského zámku 120, Troja ☎ 296 112 230 🕙 Daily
9–6, May–Sep; 9–4, rest of year 🍴 Buffet 🚇 Nádraží Holešovice,
then bus 112 to Zoologická zahrada 🎟 Moderate

KEEPING 'EM HAPPY

There are enough jazz bands,
sword-swallowers and
other entertainers on the
streets to keep children
happily staring for hours, not
to mention any number of tall
towers to climb.

For junior travellers who
prefer a more structured
experience, there are now two
Old Town wax museums, both
offering a line-up of Czech
historical and legendary
personalities. A more high-
tech attraction is the
multimedia St. Michael
Mystery, just off Staroměstské
náměstí (Old Town Square).
Visitors are guided through
the history and legends of
Prague, helped by projected
holograms, sound effects and
laser lights.

GETTING AROUND

Tram rides are a novelty to
many children—and excellent
for getting to know the city. It
is also fun to take them on
the 'train' that chugs up to
Prague Castle from Old
Town Square

Communist Mementoes

COMMUNIST CORRUPTION

Despite being lowered every evening into a refrigerated chamber and receiving the attentions of the best embalmers available, the corpse of Klement Gottwald (1896–1953, Czechoslovakia's first Communist president), in the National Memorial, continued to putrefy. When platoons of Young Pioneers were brought to admire their leader, most of what they saw was not Klement, but skillfully crafted replacement parts.

BARTOLOMĚJSKÁ POLICE STATION

The police station where Václav Havel was regularly brought in for interrogation in his dissident days has now been returned to its former owners, an order of nuns, who have leased part of it as a pension. If you book far enough ahead, you can sleep in Havel's cell.

➕ E4/5 ✉ Pension Unitas, Bartolomějská 9, Staré Město ☎ 224 211 020 🚇 Národní třída 🛗 Accessible only to pension guests

CROWNE PLAZA HOTEL

A totally authentic example of the monumental wedding-cake architecture of the Stalinist era.

➕ C2 ✉ Koulova 15, Dejvice ☎ 296 537 111 🍴 Café and restaurant 🚇 Dejvická then tram 20, 25 to Podbaba 🛗 Expensive to stay

JAN PALACH'S GRAVE, OLŠANSKÉ HŘBITOVY

The grave of student Jan Palach (➤ 45) is in the vast cemetery at Olšany. A square in the Old Town is named after him and flowers are regularly placed on the spot in Wenceslas Square where he burnt himself to death in 1969, in protest at the Soviet occupation.

➕ H–J5 ✉ Olšanské hřbitovy (Olšany cemetery), Vinohradská 🕐 Daily 8–7 🚇 Flora or Želivského 🛗 Free

MEMORIAL TO 17 NOVEMBER 1989

In an arcade on Národní, a little memorial panel of hands raised in supplication marks where 50,000 student demonstrators were attacked by riot police—an event seen as the genesis of the Velvet Revolution.

➕ E5 ✉ Národní 16, Nové Město 🚇 Národní třída 🛗 Free

THE METRO

Prague's Metro once sported a number of fine examples of Socialist-Realist art. The most visible is the mosaic of a chisel-chinned worker and his mate at Anděl station.

➕ D6 🕐 5AM–midnight 🚇 Anděl

HOME SWEET HOME

The housing blocks known as *Paneláks* are regarded with a mixture of affection and exasperation. Any accommodation is desirable in a city with an acute housing shortage, especially if it is supplied with hot and cold running water and central heating like most *paneláks*. The downside is the dreariness of the surroundings.

NÁRODNÍ PAMÁTNÍK (NATIONAL MEMORIAL)

Built in the interwar period, this slab of a building atop the steep rise to the east of the city centre served as a shrine to prominent Communist Party men. The memorial's future is uncertain.

➕ G4 ✉ U památníku, Žižkov 🚇 Florenc then uphill walk 🚌 133, 207

PANELÁKS

All around the outskirts of Prague are the monolithic housing estates composed of high-rise blocks nicknamed *paneláks*, system-built on the Soviet model from concrete panels manufactured on site.

PRAGUE
where to...

Czech Cuisine

PRICES

Expect to pay per person for dinner, excluding drinks:

£   Kč100–250
££   Kč250–700
£££   Above Kč700

All the restaurants listed are open daily for lunch and dinner unless otherwise stated.

DUMPLINGS

Love them or leave them, *knedlíky* (dumplings) are the inevitable accompaniment to much Czech cooking, adding further solidity to an already substantial cuisine. Every housewife has her prized recipe, using bread, flour, potatoes or semolina, and the homemade *knedlík* may have a lightness often absent from a restaurant's offering.

HOSPODA NA VERANDÁCH (£–££)

This large and popular restaurant is part of the Staropramen brewery. Good food and excellent fresh beer.

⊞ D6 ✉ Nádražní 84, Smíchov ☎ 257 191 200 🚇 Anděl

KLUB ARCHITEKTŮ (£–££)

This romanesque cellar next to the Bethlehem chapel has lots of vegetarian options, along with Czech staples served with a twist. There are, however, also English menus available here.

⊞ E4 ✉ Betlémské náměstí 5a, Staré Město ☎ 224 401 214 🚇 Národní třída

KOLKOVNA (£–££)

This updated take on the traditional pub near Old Town Square serves Czech staples along with pastas and salads. Great for groups, but be sure to reserve in advance.

⊞ E4 ✉ V Kolkovně 8, Staré Město ☎ 224 819 701 🚇 Staroměstská

KONVIKT (£)

A traditional Czech-style pub restaurant. The lunch crowd is mostly Czech, and the congenial owner holds court with his friends by the bar.

⊞ E5 ✉ Bartolomějská, Staré Město ☎ 602 243 151 🚇 Náměstí Republiky

MALOSTRANSKÁ BESEDA (£)

Czech food in Malá Strana Square.

⊞ D4 ✉ Malostranské náměstí 21 ☎ 257 530 428

🚊 Tram 12, 22, 23 to Malostranské náměstí

MYSLIVNA (££)

Located in a quiet street in Vinohrady, The Hunter's Lodge is worth seeking out for its delicious game dishes.

⊞ G5 ✉ Jagellonská 21, Vinohrady ☎ 226 270 209 🚇 Jiřího z Poděbrad

NA OŘECHOVCE (££)

Pub-restaurant with some of the city's best Czech food, deep in the garden suburb of Ořechovka (Walnut Grove).

⊞ B3 ✉ Východní 7, Dejvice ☎ 602 475 601 🚊 Tram 1, 2, 18 to Sibeliova

NOVOMĚSTSKÝ PIVOVAR (£)

This brewery serves up its own light and dark lagers along with traditional Czech fare.

⊞ E5 ✉ Vodičkova 20, Nové Město ☎ 222 232 448 🕐 Also open for breakfast Mon–Fri 🚊 Tram 3, 9, 14, 24 to Vodičkova

PLZEŇSKÁ RESTAURACE (££)

In the basement of the Municipal House (➤ 48) is this art-nouveau designer's idea of what a Bohemian beer hall should look like. The food is standard pub fare such as goulash.

⊞ E/F4 ✉ Náměstí Republiky 5, Staré Město ☎ 222 002 780 🚇 Náměstí Republiky

POD KŘÍDLEM (£££)

Stylish surroundings and impeccable food. Also close to the National Theatre.

⊞ E5 ✉ Národní 10 (entrance on Voršilská), Nové Město ☎ 224 951 741 🚇 Národní třída

STARÁ RADNICE (£–££)

A handy lunch-stop along the Hradčany tourist trail.
⊞ C4 ✉ Loretánská 1, Hradčany ☎ 220 511 140 🚋 Tram 22, 23 to Pražský hrad or Pohořelec

STOLETÍ (£)

When was the last time stuffed avocado made you think of Greta Garbo? Or baked turkey breast Harry Truman. At this quirky place, the dishes are all named after the famous. Czech with a twist.
⊞ E4–5 ✉ Karoliny Světlé, Staré Město ☎ 222 220 008 🚇 Národní třída

U KALICHA (££)

Thanks to the Good Soldier Švejk's patronage in Austro-Hungarian days, this place is popular with visitors from abroad familiar with the famous Czech antihero. Solid food among much Švejkian memorabilia.
⊞ E/F5/6 ✉ Na bojišti 12–14, Nové Město ☎ 224 912 557 🚇 I P Pavlova

U MATOUŠE (£)

Traditional dishes plus innovative but still authentic explorations into what Czech (and Moravian) cuisine is all about. Give 24 hours notice if you want to feast on roast duckling cooked at it really should be.
⊞ D5 ✉ Preslova 17, Smíchov ☎ 257 318 864 🚇 Anděl

U PASTÝŘKY (££)

The rustic log cabin with a big open fireplace at The Shepherdess serves up tasty Slovak meals.
⊞ F5/6 ✉ Bělehradská 15, Nusle ☎ 222 560 572 🕐 Dinner only 🚋 Tram 11, 18 to Náměstí bratří Synků

U SEDMI ŠVÁBŮ (£–££)

This is the place for a rollicking medieval feast. Sit around the big hearth or at companionable benches and dine on 'genuine' 15th-century dishes as minstrels play. Hearty Bohemian food.
⊞ C4 ✉ Jánský vršek 14, Malá Strana ☎ 257 531 455 🚋 Tram 12, 22, 23 to Malostranské náměstí

U ŠUTERŮ (£££)

A cozy place specializing in Czech treats like roast duck, roast pork and fruit dumplings.
⊞ E5 ✉ Palackého 4, Nové Město ☎ 224 947 120 🕐 Closed dinner 🚇 Můstek

U ZLATÉ HRUŠKY (£££)

The Golden Pear, in a charming rococo house in romantic Nový Svět, has an attractive outdoor section.
⊞ C4 ✉ Nový Svět 3, Hradčany ☎ 220 515 356 🚋 Tram 22, 23 to Brusnice

VLTAVA (£)

Soup, carp and trout served close to the Vltava (from which one hopes the ingredients have not been fished).
⊞ E5 ✉ Between Jiráskův most and Palackého most, Rašinovo nábřeží, Nové Město ☎ 224 922 086 🚇 Karlovo náměstí

ALIVE, ALIVE O!

Cut off from the sea, Czechs have traditionally made much of freshwater fish such as trout and carp. The huge ponds constructed in the Middle Ages in which the carp, in particular, were bred by the thousand are still very much in use. Carp make up the traditional Christmas Eve dinner, and are bought live by sharp-eyed buyers from the equally sharp dealers who set up fish tanks in the streets and squares in the days leading up to the holiday.

STILL GOING STRONG

U Modré Kachničky (£££), which translates as The Blue Duckling, was an instant success when it opened in 1993. First-rate game is served in its intimate, antiques-furnished rooms.
(⊞ D4 ✉ Nebovídská 6, Malá Strana ☎ 257 320 308 🚋 Tram 12, 22, 23 to Hellichova).

International Cuisine

CONTINENTAL

ATELIER (££)

A stylish neighbourhood eatery a bit out of the centre offering excellent fish and game.

🚼 G6 ⌧ Na Kovárně 8, Vršovice ☎ 271 721 866 🚊 Tram 4, 22, 23 to Vršovické náměstí

CAFÉ SAVOY (££)

Kafka hung out here when it was a humble café. Now a bit more upmarket, it's gaining a reputation for its French-inspired cuisine and good, fresh seafood.

🚼 D5 ⌧ Zborovská 68, Malá Strana ☎ 257 329 860 🚊 Tram 6, 9, 22, 23 to Újezd

DAVID (£££)

An intimate setting and faultless food, including melt-in-the-mouth lamb, a house speciality.

🚼 D4 ⌧ Tržiště 21, Malá Strana ☎ 257 533 109 🚊 Tram 22, 23 to Malostranské náměstí

DORBROMILA (££)

This may be one of the world's best Czech-French restaurants. The focus is on game dishes such as roast duck, rabbit in cream sauce and pheasant with wild mushrooms.

🚼 E5 ⌧ Jungmannova 10, Nové Město ☎ 296 246 464 🚇 Národní třída

KAMPA PARK (££–£££)

Stylish food in a pretty pink house on Kampa Island.

🚼 D4 ⌧ Na Kampě 8b, Malá Strana ☎ 257 532 685 🚇 Malostranská 🚊 Tram 12, 22, 23 to Malostranské náměstí

LA VERANDA (£££)

Radek David, Prague's chef of the year 2002, has created a sleek fusion of Eastern and Western cuisines. Intruiging sauces and excellent seafood.

🚼 E4 ⌧ Elišky Krásnohorské 2, Josefov ☎ 224 814 733 🚇 Staroměstská

PÁLFFY PALÁC (££–£££)

Offering serious cuisine in a comfortable atmosphere at prices that won't break the bank, this place has been a favourite among those in the know for years.

🚼 D4 ⌧ Valdštejnská 14, Malá Strana ☎ 257 530 522 🚇 Malostranská

SVATÁ KLÁRA (£££)

Dine discreetly on game, duck and other elegant fare in a cavern by the aristocratic Trojský zámek.

🚼 D1 ⌧ U trojského zámku 9 ☎ 233 540 173 🕔 Dinner only; reservations essential 🚇 Nádraží Holešovice then bus 112 to Zoologická zahrada

VAS-Y (££)

French-inspired dishes at very reasonable prices, served in a tiny bar-dining room next to the popular Globe bookshop.

🚼 E5 ⌧ Pštrossova 8, Nové Město ☎ 224 930 156 🕔 Closed Sun 🚇 Národní třída or Karlovo náměstí

ZAHRADA V OPEŘE (££)

The place to dine after attending the Státní opera. Atmospheric and delicious.

🚼 F5 ⌧ Legerova 75, Nové město (next to Radio Free Europe) ☎ 224 239 685 🚇 Muzeum

GRILLS

OPERA GRILL (£££)
Fabulous food in an intimate setting that oozes elegance.
🚇 E4 ✉ Karoliny Světlé 35, Staré Město ☎ 222 220 518 🚇 Národní třída

STAROČESKÁ KRČMA (£)
The giant open grill and candles provide the only light in this atmospheric —and aromatic—Czech place. Meat, meat and more meat.
🚇 C3 ✉ V. P. Čkalova 15, Dejvice ☎ 224 321 505 🕐 Dinner only 🚇 Dejvická

SEAFOOD

ALCRON (£££)
Hands down, Prague's premier location for seafood. Elegant.
🚇 E5 ✉ Štěpánská 40, Nové Město (in the Radisson Hotel) ☎ 224 820 038 🕐 Dinner only, closed Sun 🚇 Muzeum

NA RYBÁRNĚ (££)
Fishy delights in a restaurant supposedly once frequented by President Havel and cronies.
🚇 E5/6 ✉ Gorazdova 17, Nové Město ☎ 224 918 885 🚇 Karlovo náměstí

SUSHI BAR (££)
A tiny, stylish spot with some of Prague's best sushi. You might want to call ahead to make sure of getting fresh eel, scallops, seabass or crab as deliveries are limited.
🚇 D5 ✉ Zborovská 49a, Malá Strana ☎ 603 244 882 🚋 Tram 6, 9, 22, 23 to Újezd

AMERICAN

BAKESHOP DINER (£)
Typical diner eats plus tempting desserts.
🚇 D4 ✉ Lázeňská 19, Malá Strana ☎ 257 534 244 🚋 Tram 12, 22, 23 to Malostranské náměstí

RED HOT & BLUES (£–££)
Cajun chicken, creole gumbo and other southern specialities, plus live jazz and blues in the evenings.
🚇 E4 ✉ Jakubská 12, Staré Město ☎ 222 314 639 🚇 Náměstí Republiky

FRENCH

CHEZ MARCEL (£–££)
This comfy café/ restaurant serves up typical bistro fare. A particular favourite among expats.
🚇 E4 ✉ Haštalská 12, Staré Město ☎ 222 315 676 🚋 Tram 5, 8, 14 to Dlouhá třída

U MALÍŘŮ (£££)
The French food served in The Painter is sublime. It's in an ancient house in the middle of Malá Strana.
🚇 D4 ✉ Maltézské náměstí 11, Malá Strana ☎ 257 530 318 🚋 Tram 12, 22, 23 to Hellichova

ITALIAN

ADRIATICO (£)
Well worth the trek to the Vršovice neighbourhood for delicious homemade pastas.
🚇 H6 ✉ Moskevská 58 (entrance on Na spojce) ☎ 271 726 506 🚇 Staroměstská

LOCAL FAST FOOD

Western fast food is now available in many places, but better by far (and much cheaper) for a quick snack are the local *obložené chlebíčky* (open-faced sandwiches). Each of these is like a miniature meal, perhaps consisting of a sliver or two of ham or salami and a slice of hard-boiled egg, the whole garnished with mayonnaise and topped with pieces of pickle and red pepper.

CZECH WINES & SPIRITS

Although little known abroad, Czech wines are surprisingly good, especially both reds and whites from Moravia, and make an interesting souvenir. Spirits are cheap and often excellent. Slivovice (plum brandy) is well known, a supposed cure for all ills, while Becherovka, prepared in Carlsbad to a secret recipe, has a unique and pungent flavour.

AMICI MIECI (£££)

Italian film posters complement the elegant yet casual decor. The food is sublime.

➕ E4 ✉ Vězeňská 5, Staré Město ☎ 224 816 688 🚇 Staroměstská

CICALA (£–££)

Authentic Italian, just a block from Wenceslas Square. This is where Italian expats eat out.

➕ E5 ✉ Žitná 43, Nové Město ☎ 222 210 375 🕓 Closed Sun 🚇 Muzeum

KOGO (££)

Two locations to spot Czech celbs and politicians. The Na Příkopě location has a pleasant outdoor section.

➕ E4 ✉ Havelská 27, Staré Město ☎ 224 214 543
➕ E4 ✉ Na Příkopě 22 ☎ 221 451 259 🚇 Můstek for both

BALKAN

MODRÁ ŘEKA (£–££)

Small family-run restaurant with authentic Balkan dishes.

➕ F5 ✉ Mánesova 13, Vinohrady ☎ 222 251 601 🚇 Muzeum

OLYMPOS (££)

Enjoy roast lamb, *gyros* and other Greek specialities in the gardens.

➕ G5 ✉ Kubelíkova 9, Žižkov ☎ 222 722 239 🕓 Closed Sun 🚇 Jiřího z Poděbrad

MIDDLE EASTERN

U CEDDRU (££)

Long the port of call for those hungering for Lebanese cooking. Lamb, salads, hummus, baklava and more.

➕ C3 ✉ Na Hutich 13, Dejvice ☎ 233 342 974 🚇 Dejvická

YALLA (£)

Fast food, Middle Eastern-style. Eat in or to take-out. Many tasty treats.

➕ E4 ✉ Dlouhá 33, Staré Město ☎ 224 827 375 🚋 Tram 5, 14, 26 to Dlouhá třída

ASIAN

HANIL (££)

Generous portions of sushi meet Korean stews and grill-it-yourself dishes.

➕ G5 ✉ Slavíkova 24, Vinohrady ☎ 222 715 867 🕓 Closed Sun lunch 🚇 Jiřího z Poděbrad

HAVELI (££)

The city's best Indian food at great prices. If you like it spicy, ask them to turn up the heat.

➕ D3 ✉ Dejvocká 6, Dejvice ☎ 233 344 800 🚇 Hradčanská

ORANGE MOON (££)

See for yourself how well Czech beer complements Thai, Burmese and Indian cuisine.

➕ E4 ✉ Támjová 5, Staré Město ☎ 222 325 119 🚇 Staroměstská

SATÉ (£)

Before 1989, no Czech porker expected to end up as *satay* on a skewer but Indonesian eating has now colonized this square in upper Hradčany.

➕ C4 ✉ Pohořelec 152/3, Hradčany ☎ 220 514 552 🚋 Tram 22, 23 to Pohořelec

Vegetarian & Scenic Restaurants

VEGETARIAN

COUNTRY LIFE (£)
Healthy eating and food
shopping in the heart of
the Old Town.
🟦 E4 ✉ Melantrichova 15,
Staré Město ☎ 224 213 366
🚇 Můstek

GOVINDA
VEGETARIAN CLUB (£)
Plenty of wholefood at
this Hare Krishna
restaurant/ bakery/tea
room, in a convenient
location not far from the
art-nouveau Obecní dům
(Municipal House, ➤ 48).
🟦 F4 ✉ Soukenicka 27, Nové
Město ☎ 224 816 016
🚇 Mon–Fri 11–5 🚇 Náměstí
Republiky

LOTOS (£–££)
Refined meat-free dining
for everyone from strict
vegans to those seeking
a change from the pork-
heavy Czech diet.
🟦 E4 ✉ Platnéřská 13, Staré
Město ☎ 222 322 390
🚇 Staroměstská

RADOST CAFÉ FX
(£–££)
Trendy café; *très chic.*
🟦 F6 ✉ Bělehradská 120,
Vinohrady ☎ 224 254 776
🚇 I P Pavlova

RESTAURANTS
WITH A VIEW OR
TERRACE

BAZAAR (££)
A terrace garden looks out
over the roofs of Malá
Strana. Live music and
grilled specialities.
🟦 C4 ✉ Nerudova 40, Malá
Strana ☎ 257 535 050
🚋 Tram 12, 22, 23 to
Malostranské náměstí

HANAVSKÝ PAVILON
(£££)
The delightful little
art-nouveau Hanava
Pavilion, perched high
above the River Vltava,
serves mostly foreign
guests. It offers
continental cuisine, as
well as Bohemian game
and poultry dishes.
🟦 D3 ✉ Letenské sady 173,
Letná ☎ 233 323 641
🚋 Tram 18 to Chotkovy sady

LENTENSKÝ ZÁMEČEK
(£–££)
Large outdoor seating area
in the park where Prague
spends the summer, with
an amazing view from
the bluff.
🟦 F3 ✉ Letenské sady 341,
Holešovice ☎ 233 378 200
🚋 Tram 1, 8, 25, 26 to
Kamenická

PARNAS (£££)
For a special night out.
Sumptuous setting and
sophisticated continental
cuisine combined with an
unbeatable view of the
Vltava and Prague Castle.
To be sure of that view
reserve a window table.
🟦 D5 ✉ Smetanovo
nábřeží 2, Staré Město ☎ 224
239 604 🚇 Národní třída

PETŘINSKÉ TERSAY
(£–££)
Enjoy well-prepared
Czech specialities on the
terrace or in the winter
garden. Spectacular views
from the middle of Petřin
park.
🟦 C4 ✉ Seminářská zahrada
13, Malá Strana ☎ 257 320
688 🚇 Národní třída
🚋 Tram 12, 22, 23 to
Hellichova, then walk or take the
funicular up the hill one stop

VEGGIE REVOLUTION

Before 1989, vegetarians
venturing to Prague were
liable to be served endless
omelettes, perhaps with extra
dumplings. Czechs still like
their rich and hearty meat-
based dishes, but waiters and
others are no longer fazed
when a foreigner expresses an
interest in something else.

KOSHER FOOD

Good kosher food in an
elegant atmosphere can be
found at the King Solomon
restuarant (£££). Lovely winter
garden (🟦 E4 ✉ Široká,
Josefov ☎ 224 818 752
🚇 Staroměstská).

Pubs, Bars & Cafés

CZECH BEER

Lager beer was virtually invented in Bohemia, when the citizens of Plzeň (Pilsen) got together to form the Burghers' Brewery in 1842 and began producing the light and tasty liquid that has spawned endless imitation 'pils' ever since but which has never been surpassed. But other Czech beers are just as good, better from the barrel than the bottle. Try Prague's own Staropramen or Braník, or the milder Budvar from České Budějovice (Budweis) in southern Bohemia.

PUBS

ČERNÝ OREL

An enclosed courtyard and rustic interior lend this inn the feeling of being miles removed from the bustling city streets.
➕ D4 ✉ U Lužického semináře 40, Malá Strana ☎ 257 531 738 🚇 Malostranská

HLUČNÁ SAMOTA

A hopping neighbourhood pub dedicated to Czech writer Bohumil Hrabal, author of the novel *Too Loud a Solitude*.
➕ F6 ✉ Záhřebská 14, Vinohrady ☎ 222 522 839 🚇 Náměstí Míru

MOLLY MALONE'S

One of Prague's first Irish pubs. Guinness and great atmosphere, tucked away on a quiet back lane.
➕ E4 ✉ U obecního dvora 4, Staré Město ☎ 224 818 851 🚇 Staroměstská

PIVNICE RADEGAST

Authentic and cheap—a rare find in the touristy centre. The waiters keep bringing the beers until you tell them to stop.
➕ E4 ✉ Templova 2, Staré Město ☎ 222 328 069 🚇 Náměstí Republiky

U FLEKŮ

Every visitor should sip the dark and tasty beer that has been brewed and served on these raucous premises for 200 years. There's also a big beer garden.
➕ E5 ✉ Křemencova 11, Nové Město ☎ 224 934 019 🚇 Karlovo náměstí or Národní třída

U KOCOURA

The famous old Tomcat is a welcome sight on the hard trek up from Malá Strana to Prague Castle.
➕ D4 ✉ Nerudova 2, Malá Strana 🚊 Tram 12, 22, 23 to Malostranské náměstí

U MEDVÍDKŮ

Budvar, from the town of České Budějovice in southern Bohemia, is probably the best-known Bohemian beer apart from Pilsener. Try it here, on tap—out in the garden in summer.
➕ E4 ✉ Na Perštýně 7, Staré Město ☎ 224 211 916 🚇 Národní třída

U NOVÁKA

An updated take on the traditional Czech pub.
➕ E5 ✉ V Jirchářích 2, Nové Město ☎ 224 930 639 🚊 Tram 6, 9, 18, 21, 22, 23 to Národní divadlo

U PAŘASUTISTŮ

World War II buffs will love this pub, a shrine to the Czech parachutists who assassinated Reichsprotektor Heydrich. Across the street is the museum devoted to them, located in the Sts. Cyril and Methodius Orthodox church.
➕ E5 ✉ Resslova, 7 🚇 Karlovo náměstí

U VEJVODŮ

This former smoky old pub has been remodelled, enlarged and cleaned up, and now the Pilsner palace appeals to visitors and locals alike.
➕ E4 ✉ Jilská 4, Staré Město ☎ 224 219 999 🚇 Národní třída

CAFÉS & BARS

AU GOURMAND CAFÉ
Fresh-baked sweet and savory treats in a beautifully restored art-nouveau butcher's shop.
✚ E4 ✉ Dlouhá 10, Staré Město ☎ 222 329 060 🚇 Staroměstská

CAFÉ LOUVRE
A famous establishment now under its original name, the Louvre is decorated in rococo style and offers everything from breakfast to billiards. Also, rare for Prague, a non-smoking room.
✚ E5 ✉ Národní 20, Nové Město ☎ 224 930 949 🚇 Národní třída

CAFÉ MILENA
An elegant café in Old Town Square, with a prime view of the Orloj.
✚ E4 ✉ Staroměstské náměstí 22, Staré Město ☎ 221 632 602 🚇 Staroměstská

DOLCE VITA
Reasonably genuine Italian *caffé* with a small upper gallery for an intimate *grappa*, a busy street level and a few outdoor tables close to Old Town Square.
✚ E4 ✉ Široká 15, Staré Město ☎ 222 329 192 🚇 Staroměstská

EVROPA
It takes arrogance for a café to charge an entrance fee, as does the art-nouveau café of the Evropa Hotel. Still, the place is not to be missed.
✚ E5 ✉ Václavské náměstí 25, Nové Město ☎ 224 228 117 🚇 Můstek

IMPERIAL
Amazing art-nouveau ceramic tiling, live jazz and that once-in-a-lifetime chance to pelt fellow customers (or be pelted) with day-old doughnuts.
✚ F4 ✉ Na Poříčí 15, Nové Město ☎ 222 316 012 🚇 Náměstí Republiky

KAABA
Assortment of gourmet coffees in a cool, 1950s-modern atmosphere.
✚ F5 ✉ Mánesova 20, Vinohrady 🕐 Closed Sun ☎ 222 254 021 🚇 Muzeum

MONTMARTE
Few tourists find this cozy spot, a pre-World War II cabaret situated on a quiet street of the Old Town.
✚ E4 ✉ Řetězova 7, Staré Město 🕐 Closed Sun ☎ 222 221 244 🚇 Staroměstská

OBECNÍ DŮM
A soaring art-nouveau classic, now restored to its original brilliance.
✚ F4 ✉ Náměstí Republiky 5, Staré Město ☎ 224 239 604 🚇 Náměstí Republiky

SLAVIA
This classic Central European café, with its view over the Vltava, is open again after a long and controversial closure.
✚ D5 ✉ Smetanovo nábřeží 2, Staré Město ☎ 222 002 763 🚇 Národní třída

VELRYBA
The Whale opens wide its jaws to accommodate its trendy clientele.
✚ E5 ✉ Opatovická 24, Nové Město ☎ 224 912 484 🚇 Národní třída

TURKISH COFFEE

Espresso, cappuccino and most other coffees can now be found in Prague, but don't be surprised if you get served a traditional *'turecká káva'*. This is Czech-style Turkish coffee—that is, hot water poured right over ground coffee. Invariably served in a piping-hot glass with no handle. Be sure to stop swallowing—that is before you disturb the deposit of coffee grounds at the bottom of the cup.

71

Books & Antiques

BARGAINS... PERHAPS

Czechs are great readers, and until recently new and second-hand books were very inexpensive, many of them in languages other than Czech. Prices have risen considerably since 1989, but there are still many bargains. That said, prices for antique books are now well in line with those on the international market.

NEW BOOKS

ACADEMIA

Good variety of photography books, travel guides, cookbooks and literature in English. Run by the Academia publishing house.
➕ E5 ✉ Václavské náměstí 34, Nové Město ☎ 224 223 511 🚇 Můstek

ANAGRAM

Fiction, philosophy, religion and history in English are the specialities of this shop located in the bustling Týn Courtyard.
➕ E4 ✉ Týn 4 (between Týnská and Štupartská), Staré Město ☎ 224 895 737 🚇 Náměstí Republiky

BIG BEN

Guidebooks and Czech literature in translation are in good supply at this small shop.
➕ E4 ✉ Malá Štupartská 5, Staré Město ☎ 224 826 565 🚇 Náměstí Republiky

THE GLOBE BOOKSTORE AND COFFEEHOUSE

A congenial home-away-from-home for Americans and anyone hungry for literature in English, as well as light meals and American-style coffee.
➕ E5 ✉ Pštrossova 6, Nové Město ☎ 224 934 203 🚇 Národní třída or Karlovo náměstí

KIWI

Don't be put off by the travel agency on the ground floor; the shop in the basement has one of the best selections of maps and guides in Prague.
➕ E5 ✉ Jungmannova 23, Nové Město ☎ 296 245 500 🚇 Národní třída

KNIHKUPECTVÍ U ČERNÉ MATKY BOŽÍ

A large, well-stocked bookshop that carries a good selection of coffee-table books in English. Unmissable location in the Cubist House at the Black Madonna (► 58).
➕ E4 ✉ Celetná 34, Staré Město ☎ 224 211 275 🚇 Náměstí Republiky

SHAKESPEARE & SONS

A bookshop/café featuring new and used books and magazines, including a good selection of Czech authors in translation.
➕ G6 ✉ Krymská 12, Vršovice ☎ 271 740 839 🚊 Tram 4, 22, 23 to Krymská

ANTIQUES & ANTIQUARIAN BOOKSHOPS

ANTIKVARIÁT EVA KOZÁKOVÁ

Old photographs, prints and postcards, plus innumerable old books, mostly Czech.
➕ E5 ✉ Myslíkova 10, Nové Město ☎ 224 917 862 🚇 Karlovo náměstí

ART DECO

Glass, ceramics, clothing, jewellery and more from the 1920s and 30s.
➕ E4 ✉ Michalská 21, Staré Město ☎ 224 223 076 🚇 Národní třída

DOROTHEUM

This branch of the long-established Vienna auction house has a fine range of antiques of all kinds. No bargains, but no rip-offs either.

🟥 E4 ✉ Ovocný trh 2, Staré Město ☎ 224 222 001
🔵 Můstek or Náměstí Republiky

EX LIBRIS

Intriguing second-hand books of Czech art and photography, plus many art books in German and English.

🟥 E4-5 ✉ Konviktská 6, Staré Město ☎ 224 235 451
🔵 Národní třída

FOTO ŠKODA

Together with Jan Pazdera's shop across the street at Vodičkova 28, a veritable paradise for camera buffs and collectors. Huge selection of communist-bloc models such as Praktina and Kiev.

🟥 E5 ✉ Vodičkova 37, Nové Město ☎ 224 217 129
🔵 Můstek

GALERIE–ANTIKVARIÁT U BÍLÉHO ZAJÍCE

Old and modern prints, posters, all manner of ephemera and books.

🟥 E4 ✉ Michalská 15, Staré Město ☎ 224 231 119
🔵 Národní třída

HODINÁŘSTVÍ VÁCLAV MATOUŠ

Beautiful antique clocks and watches, still ticking.

🟥 E5 ✉ Mikulandská 10, Nové Město ☎ 224 930 172
🔵 Národní třída

NA STARÉ POŠTĚ

The specialities here are 19th- and 20th-century Czech paintings and old dolls and puppets. A few pieces of Rosenthal and Pirkenhammer porcelain

and such oddities as walking sticks add to the mix.

🟥 D5 ✉ Maltézské náměstí 8, Malá Strana ☎ 257 530 317
🚋 Tram 12, 22, 23 to Hellichova

PRAŽSKÉ STAROŽITNOSTI

'Prague Antiques' sells jewellery, porcelain and paintings galore.

🟥 E5 ✉ Mikulandská 8, Nové Město ☎ 224 930 572
🔵 Národní třída

STAROŽITNICTVÍ U ZLATÉ ULIČKY

A good selection of jewellery and other antiques at reasonable prices. Just around the corner from Prague Castle's Golden Lane.

🟥 D4 ✉ U Daliborky 30/31 ☎ 223 339 875 🚋 Tram 22, 23 to Pražský hrad

SYMPOSIUM

This antiquarian/auction house offers rare books and manuscripts dating from the 15th to 20th centuries, plus maps, prints and more.

🟥 C–D4 ✉ Vlašská 11, Malá Strana ☎ 607 266 517
🚋 Tram 12, 22, 23 to Malostranské náměstí

ZLATÁ KORUNA

Antique coins, medals and paper money.

🟥 E4 ✉ Pařížská 8, Staré Město ☎ 222 319 689
🔵 Staroměstská

ZLATNICTVÍ VOMÁČKA

Antique and second-hand jewellery, porcelain and diverse knick-knacks.

🟥 E4 ✉ Náprstkova 9, Staré Město ☎ 222 222 017
🔵 Národní třída

WENCESLAS HOLLAR

One of the first artists to make accurate drawings of the English landscape was Wenceslas Hollar. Born in 1607 in Bohemia, Václav (to give him his Czech name) sought refuge abroad following the Protestant defeat at the Battle of the White Mountain and was employed as a draftsman by the Earl of Arundel. A trawl through Prague's antiquarian bookshops might turn up a Hollar original, such as his wonderfully detailed 1636 panorama of the city, but there are plenty of alternatives by other artists—drawings, engravings and maps—at affordable prices.

Gifts, Souvenirs & Music

KAFKA AT HOME

One of the many places lived in by novelist Franz Kafka was the house on Celetná Street adjoining Kostel Panny Marie Před Týnem (Týn Church). In the bedroom in which Kafka slept and dreamed as a child, a blank window faces down the south aisle of the church's nave.

SGRAFFITO

The Schwarzenberský palác (Schwarzenberg Palace) on Hradčanské náměstí is probably Prague's most splendidly sgraffitoed building. Sgraffito work involves picking out patterns in two shades of plasterwork either to accentuate the architectural character of the building or to cover the façade with lively pictures, as in Martinický palác (Martinic Palace) and Hradčany Square.

TOYS, PUPPETS & SOUVENIRS

CLASSIC MODEL

New and second-hand trains galore, including rarities dating from the Communist era.
➕ D5 ✉ Bartolomějská 3, Staré Město 🚇 Národní třída

FIRMA AMI

Some of the finest hand-made puppets available in Prague. Some individual designs can be expensive but others are reasonably priced. Supplied by over 30 different craftsmen.
➕ C4 ✉ Nerudova 51, Malá Strana 🚇 Malostranská

IVRE

Lots of locally made soft toys and hand puppets.
➕ E4 ✉ Jakubská 3, Staré Město ☎ 222 326 644 🚇 Náměstí Republiky

KID-TRNKA

Sensible and imaginative wooden toys.
➕ E5 ✉ Ostrovní 21, Nové Město ☎ 224 930 858 🚇 Národní třída.

KOŽESNICTVÍ KREIBICH

Central Eruopeans still wear their furs without shame. This small shop, which carries a variety of hats, gloves and coats, and caters mostly to a Czech clientele.
➕ E4 ✉ Michalská 14, Staré Město ☎ 224 222 522 🚇 Národní třída

MANUFAKTURA

Natural goods and traditional handicrafts, including linens, blankets, wooden toys and Christmas ornaments.
➕ E4 ✉ Melantrichova 17, Staré Město ☎ 221 632 411 🚇 Můstek

MUSEUM SHOP

Unusually tasteful and original souvenirs based on the treasures of the many Prague museums, plus foreign art books not available elsewhere in Prague. An example to other souvenir shops worldwide; where else, for example, could you buy a china mug with elegant sgraffito patterning?
➕ D4 ✉ Jiřská 6, Hradčany ☎ 224 373 264 🚊 Tram 22, 23 to Pražský hrad

OBCHOD S LOUTKAMI

Head here when not just any marionette will do. These two shops feature unique, top quality pieces of art.
➕ C4 ✉ Nerudova 47 and 51, Malá Strana ☎ 257 533 035 🚊 Tram 12, 22, 23 to Malostranské náměstí

POHÁDKA

This store, whose name means Fairy Tale, sells the usual cast of characters in a wide variety of finger puppets and marionettes.
➕ E4 ✉ Celetná 32, Staré Město 🚇 Náměstí Republiky

ARTS & CRAFTS

BOTANICUS

Organic products—soap, cosmetics, teas, herbs and spices—produced on a farm in Lysá nad Labem.
➕ E4 ✉ Michalská 2, Staré Město ☎ 224 212 977 🚇 Můstek

CASHPI

Designer glassware, a Czech speciality.

➕ E4 ✉ Celetná 19, Staré Město ☎ 224 812 713 🚇 Náměstí Republiky

CELETNÁ CRYSTAL

Sells good-quality Bohemian glass.

➕ E4 ✉ Celetná 15, Staré Město 🚇 Náměsti Republiky

GALERIE PEITHNER-LICHTENFELS

Modern Czech and Austrian art, including works from the period between the wars.

➕ E4 ✉ Michalská 12, Staré Město ☎ 224 227 680 🚇 Můstek

GALERIE PYRAMIDA

Not all Czech glass is for serving wine in. This spacious shop displays art glass from some of the best Czech designers. Good-quality small bronzes and other objets d'art are also sold.

➕ E5 ✉ Národní 11, Nové Město ☎ 224 213 117 🚇 Národní třída

GRANÁT

Bohemian garnets are world-famous; this factory shop has the most varied selection.

➕ E4 ✉ Dlouhá 30, Staré město ☎ 222 315 612 🚇 Náměstí Republiky

IVANA FOLLOVÁ ART AND FASHION

A large shop in the Týn courtyard offering high quality, locally made silk dresses and scarves, jewellery and ceramics.

➕ E4 ✉ Týn 1 (between Týnská and Štupartská), Staré

Město ☎ 224 895 460 🚇 Náměstí Republiky

MOSER

The outlet for the fine crystal and porcelain made in Carlsbad (Karlovy Vary), plus porcelain from Meissen and Herend.

➕ E4 ✉ Na příkopě 12, Staré Město ☎ 224 211 293 🚇 Můstek or Náměstí Republiky

SKLO BOHEMIA

Bohemian glassware from Světlá nad Sázavou.

➕ E4 ✉ Na příkopě 17 ☎ 224 239 653 🚇 Můstek or Náměstí Republiky

MUSIC

AGHARTA

Jazz, jazz and more jazz on sale at this popular nightspot.

➕ F5 ✉ Krakovská 5, Nové Město 🕐 Evenings only 🚇 Muzeum

BONTONLAND KORUNA

Reputedly the biggest music shop in Central Europe, although better for pop and rock than classical music. In the labyrinthine basement of the Koruna Palace at the corner of Wenceslas Square and Na příkopě.

➕ E4 ✉ Václavské náměstí 1, Nové Město ☎ 224 473 080 🚇 Můstek

KAFKOVO KNIHKUPECTVÍ

Traditional folk music, from *klezmer* to gypsy to oom-pah, plus classical and jazz.

➕ E4 ✉ Staroměstské náměstí 12, Staré Město ☎ 222 321 454 🚇 Staroměstská

MUSICAL MISCELLANY

In addition to excellent CDs of music by the classical composers most closely associated with the city (Mozart, Dvořák, Smetana...), Prague shops stock strongly flavoured and highly individual pop music (Šum Svistu, or Laura and her Tigers, Psi vojáci...). Even more distinctive are the brass bands—the best you've ever heard—pumping out Czech (yes, Czech) old-time favourites such as 'Roll Out the Barrel' (*Škoda lásky*).

Department Stores, Markets & Food

RED ARMY SURPLUS

After 1989, the Warsaw Pact crumbled and the Red Army began its long retreat back to Moscow, shedding its surplus equipment as it went. Many Czech farmers now carry a Kalashnikov rifle rather than a humble shotgun, while visitors may still find themselves tempted by the trim greatcoats or the improbably high-peaked officers' caps that are on sale wherever tourists congregate.

DEPARTMENT STORES

BÍLÁ LABUŤ

The White Swan is a long-established department store on an unfashionable but interesting shopping street just east of the Old Town. A branch is now open on Wenceslas Square opposite the National Museum.
➕ F4 ☒ Na Poříčí 23, north Nové Město Ⓜ Náměstí Republiky

KOTVA

The Anchor was completed in 1975 and for a while was the city's foremost shopping site, though the range of goods would have seemed basic to Western consumers. Nowadays, many department stores are independent and well-stocked, while others just offer the basics, from pillows to pans to paper.
➕ E4 ☒ Náměstí Republiky 8, Staré Město Ⓜ Náměstí Republiky

KRONE

A German equivalent of Tesco, on Wenceslas Square.
➕ E4 ☒ Václavské náměstí 21 Ⓜ Můstek

TESCO

Rival to Kotva and once bearing the impeccably proletarian name of 'Máj' (May), this department store is now in British hands. A ride up the escalator gives an excellent view of the city centre.
➕ E5 ☒ Národní 26, Nové Město Ⓜ Národní třída

MARKETS

HAVELSKÁ/ V KOTCÍCH

Atmospheric market for fruits, vegetables and souvenirs.
➕ E4 ☒ Staré Město Ⓒ Daily Ⓜ Můstek

HOLEŠOVICKÁ TRŽNICE

Comprehensive market on the far side of the Vltava, north of Old Town.
➕ G3 ☒ Bubenské nábřeží, Holešovice Ⓒ Closed Sunday 🚊 Tram 1, 3, 14, 25 to Holešovická tržnice

PRAŽSKÁ BURZA

Cheap clothes, motor parts and an abundance of things you won't want. Fascinating spectacle.
➕ F2 ☒ Výstaviště (Exhibition Grounds), Holešovice Ⓒ Sat–Sun 10–2 🚊 Tram 5, 12, 17 to Výstaviště

FOOD SHOPS

COUNTRY LIFE

Healthy natural foods—elsewhere hard to find in this calorie-addicted city.
➕ E4 ☒ Melantrichova 15, Staré město Ⓜ Můstek

FRUITS DE FRANCE

French Fruits changed the face of food shopping in Prague not long after the Velvet Revolution, and is still the place for classy imported foods.
➕ E4 ☒ Jindřišská 9, Nové Město Ⓜ Můstek

UZENINY

Every kind of Central European sausage.
➕ E4 ☒ Na Můstku 8 Ⓜ Můstek

Opera & Church Concerts

OPERA

HUDEBNÍ DIVADLO V KARLÍNĚ (KARLÍN MUSICAL THEATRE)

Operettas and musicals are the undemanding fare in this theatre. Due to flooding, performances are being held at the Congress Centre.

Congress Centre: **F7**
✉ Společensk sál (entrance 5), trida 5, Kvetna, Pankrác
☎ 261 174 400 📍 Vyšehrad
Karlin Theatre: **F4**
✉ Křižíkova 10, Karlin
☎ 221 868 149 📍 Florenc

NÁRODNÍ DIVADLO (NATIONAL THEATRE)

Operas from both the Czech and international repertoire are performed in a sumptuous setting in the National Theatre (► 38).

STÁTNÍ OPERA PRAHA (STATE OPERA)

Opened in 1887 as the Deutsches Theater (German Theatre), this neo-Renaissance building became the Smetanovo divadlo (Smetana Theatre) after World War II. It's now the State Opera, with performances from the international repertoire and classical ballet.

F5 ✉ Wilsonova 4, Nové Město ☎ 224 227 266 📍 Muzeum

STAVOVSKÉ DIVADLO (ESTATES THEATRE)

The venue that saw the premiere of Mozart's *Don Giovanni* in 1787 is a marvel of pristine neoclassical glory.

Regular performances of Wolfgang's greatest hits can be enjoyed here.

E4 ✉ Ovocný trh, Staré Město ☎ 224 901 448 📍 Můstek

CONCERTS IN CHURCHES

BAZILIKA SV JIŘÍ (ST. GEORGE'S BASILICA)

The castle's austere Romanesque church is now used for chamber concerts (► 33).

CHRÁM SV MIKULÁŠE (ST. NICHOLAS'S CHURCH), MALÁ STRANA

The organ that Mozart played in Prague's greatest baroque church still accompanies choral concerts (► 35).

KOSTEL SV JAKUBA (ST. JAMES'S CHURCH)

The admirable acoustics in this Old Town church augment the concerts of sacred music held here (► 57).

KOSTEL SV JILJÍ (ST. GILES'S CHURCH)

Regular organ concerts in the sanctuary and strings in the chapel.

E4 ✉ Husova 6, Staré Město 📍 Národní třída

KOSTEL SV MIKULÁŠE, STARÉ MĚSTO (ST. NICHOLAS'S CHURCH, OLD TOWN)

The other Church of St. Nicholas is less sumptuous than the one in Malá Strana but an equally fine choice for organ and vocal recitals (► 57).

MOZART IN PRAGUE

'My Praguers understand me', declared Mozart, who was far better received here than in Vienna. Both *Figaro* and *Don Giovanni* were hits in Prague, and after his pauper's death in Vienna, it was Prague that honoured him with a great funeral mass in Malá Strana's St. Nicholas's Church, attended by a crowd of 4,000 mourners.

Concerts in Other Venues

JOSEF KAJETÁN TYL

The Stavovské divadlo (Estates Theatre, ➤ 77) reverted to its original name in 1991. For many years it was called the Tyl Theatre; almost unknown abroad, the 19th-century playwright Josef Kajetán Tyl is dear to Czech hearts for his comedy *Fidlovačka*, which contains the song *'Kde domov můj?'* ('Where is my home?'), a plaintive call that later was adopted as the Czech national anthem.

ATRIUM NA ŽIŽKOVĚ

Concert hall featuring Italian baroque music, ensembles of historical instruments, *klezmer* and other unique stlyes.

➕ G5 ✉ Cajkovského 12, Žižkov ☎ 222 721 838
🚊 Tram 5, 9, 26 to Lipanská

BERTRAMKA (MOZART MUSEUM)

Mozart's Prague patrons, the Dušeks, once lived here and it is where the composer finished *Don Giovanni*. The museum (➤ 55) stages regular concerts.

CLAM-GALLASŮV PALÁC (CLAM-GALLAS PALACE)

Chamber concerts in a gargantuan Old Town mansion otherwise rarely open to the public.

➕ E4 ✉ Husova 20, Staré Město 🚇 Staroměstská

KLEMENTINUM

This vast complex hosts chamber concerts in its Hall of Mirrors (Zrcadlová síň).

➕ E4 ✉ Entrances at Karlova 1, Mariánské náměstí and Křížovnické náměstí, Staré Město 🚇 Staroměstská

LICHTENŠTEJNSKÝ PALÁC (LIECHTENSTEIN PALACE)

Palatial setting for symphonic and other performances. The home of the Prague Music academy where students perform regularly.

➕ D4 ✉ Malostranské náměstí 13, Malá Strana ☎ 257 534 206 🚊 Tram 12, 22, 23 to Malostranské náměstí

LOBKOVICKÝ PALÁC (LOBKOVIC PALACE)

Chamber concerts in the banqueting hall of a palace near the castle precinct.

➕ D4 ✉ Jiřská 3, Hradčany ☎ 233 354 457
🚇 Malostranská then uphill walk 🚊 Tram 22, 23 to Pražský hrad

RUDOLFINUM

The Dvořák Hall of this splendid neo-Renaissance hall on the Vltava is the home of the Czech Philharmonic Orchestra. The Little (or Suk) Hall is used for chamber concerts.

➕ E4 ✉ Náměstí Jana Palacha, Staré Město ☎ 227 059 352 🚇 Staroměstská

SMETANOVA SÍŇ (SMETANA HALL)

Part of the sumptuously decorated Municipal House, and home of the Prague Symphony Orchestra (➤ 59).

TROJSKÝ ZÁMEK (TROJA CHÂTEAU)

The magnificence of Count Šternberg's out-of-town palace almost overwhelms the music (➤ 50).

VALDŠTEJNSKÝ PALÁC (WALLENSTEIN PALACE)

Wonderful summer evening concerts in the baroque gardens (➤ 36).

VILA AMERIKA

Count Michna's jolly little 18th-century summer palace, home of the Dvořák Museum, stages tributes to the composer's life and work (➤ 59).

Pop & Rock

CLUB MECCA

Local DJs and guests from Europe's leading dance palaces spin records in this club out in a gentrifying industrial district. The adjacent restaurant attracts a similarly style-conscious crowd.

➕ G2 ✉ U Průhonu 3, Holešovice ☎ 283 870 522 🚊 Vltavská, then tram 1, 3, 14, 25 to Dělnická

LÁVKA

Come here for dancing to recorded music on the riverside close to Prague's most celebrated bridge, Karlův most (Charles Bridge).

➕ D4 ✉ Novotného lávka 1, Staré Město ☎ 222 222 156 🚊 Staroměstská

LUCERNA MUSIC BAR

This is part of the vast complex of the Lucerna Palace, a labyrinth of arcades and passageways that were the work of President Havel's builder-grandfather. Its good-sized ballroom can accommodate visiting groups as well as locals, and although some expats look down on it, it's the place to go for Czech retro.

➕ E5 ✉ Vodičkova 36, Nové Město ☎ 224 217 108 🚊 Můstek

MALOSTRANSKÁ BESEDA

Something for everyone—ska, folk, reggae, blues, rock. You might even catch the Original Prague Syncopated Orchestra, with its immaculate re-creation of vintage swing. Before or after the music you can relax in the café-cum-gallery that also occupies the premises.

➕ D4 ✉ Malostranské náměstí 21, Malá Strana ☎ 257 532 092 🚊 Malostranská 🚊 Tram 22, 23 to Malostranské náměstí

PALÁC AKROPOLIS

In the shadow of the television tower (➤ 53), this is the city's main venue for world music and alternative acts. There's a dance club, too. The funky pub on the premises is popular with younger expats and locals.

➕ G5 ✉ Kubelíkova 27, Žižkov ☎ 296 330 913 🚊 Jiřího z Poděbrad

RADOST FX

A serious dance scene prevails at one of the city's most well-known clubs. Trendy spot.

➕ F6 ✉ Bělehradská 120, Vinohrady ☎ 224 254 776 🚊 I P Pavlova

ROCK CAFÉ

This city-centre café and concert spot is the place to go if you like your rock music hard and very loud.

➕ E5 ✉ Národní 20, Nové Město ☎ 224 914 414 🚊 Národní třída

ROXY

Unusual underground establishment that has DJs and live acts of every conceivable stripe, including stars of world music.

➕ E4 ✉ Dlouhá 33, Staré Město ☎ 224 826 296 🚊 Náměstí Republiky

ROCK CZECH-STYLE

Before 1989, groups like the Plastic People of the Universe were seen as genuinely subversive of the existing order and were relentlessly hounded by State Security. Nowadays, the rock scene is a confused one, with a lot of fairly mindless imitation of Western trends but some innovation too, by groups like Šum Svistu (Latin influenced) and Shalom (obsessed by Judaism).

Jazz, Cabaret & Casinos

PRAGUE JAZZ

Jazz has deep roots among the Czech people, as evidenced in the novels and short stories of the long-exiled writer Josef Škvorecký (for example, *The Bass Saxophone*). The Prague jazz scene is highly concentrated, with most venues clustered in the area between the Národní divadlo (National Theatre) and Václavské náměstí (Wenceslas Square).

JAZZ

AGHARTA JAZZ CENTRUM
Cramped but enjoyable for local and international jazz, with cocktails and snacks. CD shop.
✚ F5 ✉ Krakovská 5, Nové Město ☎ 222 211 275 Ⓜ Muzeum

JAZZ CLUB U STARÉ PANÍ
Some of the best local musicians play in this central jazz club.
✚ E4 ✉ Michalská 9, Staré Město ☎ 224 228 090 Ⓜ Můstek

JAZZ CLUB ŽELEZNÁ
Another minuscule club for jazzers, this one is in ancient cellars in the heart of the Old Town. The music varies from swing to blues to Latin.
✚ E4 ✉ Železná 16, Staré Město ☎ 224 239 697 Ⓜ Můstek

METROPOLITAN
Swing, ragtime and blues.
✚ E5 ✉ Jungmannova 14, Nové Město ☎ 224 947 777 Ⓜ Národní třída or Můstek

REDUTA
Bill Clinton blew his sax at this best-known of Prague jazz locales during his presidential visit to Prague in 1994. You can hear Dixieland, swing and modern jazz.
✚ E5 ✉ Národní 20, Nové Město ☎ 224 933 487 Ⓜ Národní třída

U MALÉHO GLENA
Little Glenn's is named after its genial owner, who provides recorded jazz in the candlelit upstairs bar and the real thing—alternating with pop and rock—in the tiny basement.
✚ D4 ✉ Karmelitská 23, Malá Strana ☎ 257 531 717 Ⓣ Tram 12, 22, 23 to Malostranské náměstí

UNGELT JAZZ 'N' BLUES CLUB
More pub than club, this newish place concentrates on local talent.
✚ E4 ✉ Týn 2 (enter from Týnská ulička), Staré Město ☎ 224 895 748 Ⓜ Můstek or Staroměstská

CASINOS & CABARETS

If you want to see a good old-fashioned floor show, with music, dancing and spectacle, the larger hotels are the best bet. Reserve ahead.

CASINO HILTON ATRIUM
Roulette and other games, in spacious, modern surroundings.
✚ F3 ✉ Prague Hilton Atrium, Pobřežní 1, Karlín ☎ 224 842 005 Ⓜ Florenc

CASINO PALAIS SAVARIN
Roulette and other games.
✚ E4 ✉ Na příkopě 10, Nové Město ☎ 224 221 648 Ⓜ Můstek or Náměstí Republiky

VARIETÉ PRAGA
Variety, brass bands and gaming in a wonderful building in art-nouveau style.
✚ E5 ✉ Vodičkova 30, Nové Město ☎ 224 222 098 Ⓜ Můstek

Multimedia Theatre & Mime

Leaving aside the thriving Czech-language dramatic theatre, there's still plenty to choose from. You don't have to speak Czech to enjoy mime and multimedia (known locally as black light theatre), big on the Prague stage, which entertains the crowds nightly. Most shows are for foreign visitors, who can also enjoy performances of Czech folk art at various locations.

ČERNÉ DIVADLO JIŘÍHO SRNCE (JIŘÍ SRNEC BLACK THEATRE)

Legends of magic Prague presented in multimedia format.

➕ E4 ✉ Celetná 17, Staré Město ☎ 257 921 835 🚇 Náměstí Republiky

Also at ➕ E5 ✉ Divadlo Reduta, Národní třída 20, Nové Město 🚇 Národní třída

DIVADLO IMAGE (IMAGE THEATRE)

Visitor-oriented theatre with black light shows, featuring dance, mime and music.

➕ E4 ✉ Pařížská 4, Staré Město ☎ 222 314 448 🚇 Staroměstská

DIVADLO MIMŮ ALFRED VE DVOŘE (ALFRED IN THE COURTYARD MIME THEATRE)

Ctibor Turba's mime troupe no longer performs here, but the suburban venue hosts occasional visiting performers.

➕ F3 ✉ Františka Křižka 36, Holešovice ☎ 233 376 997 🚊 Tram 5, 12, 17 to Veletržní

KONGRESOVÉ CENTRUM (CONGRESS CENTRE)

Big-budget Czech-language musicals and other events are staged in the city's largest auditorium, once the gathering place for Communist Party bigwigs.

➕ F7 ✉ 5 května 1640/65, Vyšehrad ☎ 261 174 444 🚇 Vyšehrad

LATERNA MAGIKA

The Magic Lantern's synthesis of film, music, theatre and mime was first developed in the 1950s by Alfréd Radok, and continues to intrigue and delight audiences. Some of the most successful shows are reworkings of ancient myths.

➕ D/E5 ✉ Nová scéna of the National Theatre, Národní 4, Nové Město ☎ 224 931 482 🚇 Národní třída

PONEC DANCE THEATRE

This theatre is steadily gaining a reputation as the place to see modern dance.

➕ G4 ✉ Husitská 24a, Žižkov ☎ 224 817 886 🚊 Tram 5, 9, 26 to Husinecká

TA FANTASTIKA

Another spectacle based on the black light fusion of dance, mime and music – a spin-off from the hugely successful and famous Laterna Magika. The stage also hosts pop musicals starring local idols.

➕ E4 ✉ Karlova 8, Staré Město ☎ 222 221 366 🚇 Staroměstská

KEEPING YOU POSTED

Since 1989 there has been a boom in performances of all kinds intended to appeal to foreign visitors. Posters and leaflets will keep you up to date about what's on, as will the English-language *Prague Post* weekly newspaper.

CINEMA

Prague has dozens of cinemas, many around Wenceslas Square. Most are in the original version with Czech subtitles.

Drama & Puppetry

CZECH PUPPETRY

In a country where the art of manipulating marionettes is taught in universities, no one whose imagination has been stimulated by the array of delightful little figures on sale on stalls and in shops should miss one of Prague's puppet performances. The colourful characters are mostly drawn from the fairy tales that are such a feature of Czech popular literature. They include water sprites and witches, devils, soldiers and highwaymen, villains and virgins.

DIVADLO ARCHA (ARCHA THEATRE)

Archa hosts superb productions of avant-garde theatre. Tickets for most shows are inexpensive and highly sought after.

🕂 F4 ✉ Na poříčí 26, north Nové Město ☎ 221 716 333 🚇 Náměstí Republiky

DIVADLO JIŘÍHO GROSSMANNA (JIŘÍ GROSSMANN THEATRE)

Some non-Czech performances are put on in this establishment in Wenceslas Square.

🕂 E5 ✉ Vádavské náměstí 43, Nové Město ☎ 224 228 814 🚇 Můstek

DIVADLO MINOR (MINOR THEATRE)

This well-known children's puppetry and drama ensemble currently operates from the Comedy Theatre, with occasional shows elsewhere.

🕂 E5 ✉ Vodičkova 6, Nové Město ☎ 222 231 351 🚇 Můstek

DIVADLO NA ZÁBRADLÍ (THEATRE ON THE BALUSTRADE)

Václav Havel shifted scenery here. Later, his plays helped build the theatre's reputation.

🕂 E4 ✉ Anenské náměstí 5, Staré Město ☎ 222 222 026 🚇 Staroměstská

DIVADLO SPEJBLA A HURVÍNKA (SPEJBL AND HURVÍNEK THEATRE)

Don't miss the antics of Prague's immortal puppet duo: Josef Skupa's troubled father and his perky son have been performing in their own theatre since 1945.

🕂 C3 ✉ Dejvická 38, Dejvice ☎ 224 316 784 🚇 Dejvická

DIVADLO V CELETNÉ (CELETNÁ THEATRE)

The most frequent venue for shows by Prague's two resident English-language ensembles, Black Box and Misery Loves Company. The Jiří Srnec Black Theatre also performs here (► 81).

🕂 E4 ✉ Celetná 17, Staré Město ☎ 222 326 843 🚇 Náměsti Republiky

GLOBE THEATRE

In the summertime, Shakespeare is staged in Prague's own low-budget replica of The Bard's home stage. Some productions are performed in English.

🕂 E/F2 ✉ Výstaviště (Exhibition Grounds), Holešovice ☎ 220 103 608 🚋 Tram 5, 12, 17 to Výstaviště

NÁRODNÍ DIVADLO (NATIONAL THEATRE)

You can see classics of Czech theatre here, as well as performances of opera and ballet.

🕂 D/E5 ✉ Národní 2, Nové Město ☎ 224 901 448 🚇 Národní třída

NÁRODNÍ DIVADLO MARIONET (NATIONAL MARIONETTE THEATRE)

Adaptations of operas are among the attractions. There are matinees for youngsters.

🕂 E4 ✉ Žatecká 1, Staré Město ☎ 224 819 322 🚇 Můstek

Sport & Outdoor Activities

FOOTBALL

SPARTA STADIUM

First-class football at the home of Sparta Praha, one of the country's leading teams, who take part in European competitions. Tickets are easily available at the gate.
➕ E3 ✉ Milady Horákové 98, Holešovice ☎ 296 111 111 🚋 Tram 26 to Sparta

ICE HOCKEY

T-MOBILE

This big indoor venue is the base of H C Sparta Praha ice hockey team.
➕ F2 ✉ Výstaviště (Exhibition Grounds), Holešovice ☎ 266 727 443 🚋 Tram 5, 12, 17 to Výstaviště

SKATING

ŠTVANICE

One of several indoor ice rinks in Prague. In winter there's also skating on ponds, lakes and reservoirs on the outskirts of Prague.
➕ F3 ✉ Ostrov Štvanice 1125 (Štvanice Island), Holešovice ☎ 233 378 327 🚋 Tram 3, 26 to Těšnov

SWIMMING

HOSTIVAŘ RESERVOIR

Windsurfing, swimming and boating, on Prague's biggest reservoir.
➕ Off map, 12km (7.5 miles) southeast of Prague 🚇 Háje, then walk or bus 165, 170, 212

PLAVECKÝ STADION PODOLÍ (PODOLÍ POOLS)

Large complex of pools, sauna and such.

➕ E8 ✉ Podolská 74, Podolí ☎ 241 433 952 🚋 Tram 3, 17 to Kublov

SLAPY DAM & LAKE

The Vltava upstream from Prague has been dammed to form a chain of lakes with beaches made of imported sand.
➕ Off map, 32km (20 miles) south of Prague 🚌 Bus from Na Knížecí bus station (Metro Anděl)

BIKING

PRAHA BIKE

Centrally located bicycle rentals, city rides and out-of-town trips.
➕ E4 ✉ Dlouhá 24, Staré Město ☎ 732 388 880 🚇 Staroměstská

HORSE RACING

ZÁVODIŠTĚ CHUCHLE (CHUCHLE RACECOURSE)

Flat races and trotting.
➕ Off map, 10km (6 miles) south of Prague ☎ 257 941 042 🚆 Suburban train from Smíchov to Velká Chuchle 🚌 Bus 172

GOLF

GOLF CLUB PRAHAL

A basic nine-hole course in the western suburbs.
➕ Off map, 6km (3.5 miles) west of the city centre. Plzeňská 215, Motol ☎ 257 216 584 🚇 Anděl then tram 4, 7, 9 to the Hotel Golf stop

KARLŠTEJN

One of a number of newish courses; this one has the benefit of Hrad Karlštejn (Karlštejn Castle, ➤ 20) as a backdrop.
➕ Off map, 32km (20 miles) to the southwest ☎ 311 684 716

IN-TOWN CYCLING

Cycling is not particularly popular in this fume- and cobble-ridden city. On weekends urban cyclists congregate in the city's extensive Stromovka Park, where there is a network of marked cycle paths and some signposting indicating how cyclists might reach other parts of Prague in relative safety.

Luxury Hotels

PRICES

Expect to pay Kč5,000 or more for a double room in a luxury hotel.

RESERVE AHEAD

Until recently, Prague suffered from an acute shortage of hotel accommodation, particularly in the middle price range, and was not an inexpensive place to stay. The situation has improved, but it is always wise to book well in advance, especially in summer and if you want to stay in the centre.

ADRIA

A stunningly restored old establishment set amid the glitter and bustle of Wenceslas Square. With 88 rooms.

➕ E5 ✉ Václavské náměstí 26 ☎ 221 081 111; fax 221 081 300 🚇 Můstek

HOFFMEISTER

In a refurbished historic building, this luxurious 39-room hotel prides itself on its personalized service. It is enviably sited on the road up to Prague Castle.

➕ D3 ✉ Pod bruskou 7 ☎ 251 017 111; fax 251 017 120 🚇 Malostranská

INTERCONTINENTAL

This 364-room hotel was the epitome of pretension in Communist days and hypermodern when it opened back in the 1970s. Near Josefov, it has every comfort, as well as spacious public rooms furnished with antiques.

➕ E3 ✉ Náměstí Curieových 5 ☎ 296 631 111; fax 224 811 216; www.pragueinterconti.com 🚇 Staroměstská

JALTA

The air-conditioned 94-room Jalta is a fine example of 1950s architecture, and has an unbeatable position towards the top of Wenceslas Square.

➕ F5 ✉ Václavské náměstí 45 ☎ 222 822 126; fax 224 123 866 🚇 Muzeum or Můstek

JOSEF

This design hotel features 110 rooms of cool luxury and every conceivable amenity.

➕ E4 ✉ Rybná 20, Staré Město ☎ 221 700 111; fax 221 700 999; www.hoteljosef.com 🚊 Tram 5, 14, 26 to Dlouhá třída

NERUDA

Any closer to the castle and you'd be sleeping with the president. This modern yet comfy 20-room hotel is housed in a 1348 building.

➕ C4 ✉ Nerudova 44, Malá Strana ☎ 257 535 557; fax 257 531 492; www.hotelneruda-praha.cz 🚊 Tram 12, 22, 23 to Malostranské náměstí

PALACE

A sumptuous art-nouveau exterior conceals the refurbished and eminently comfortable interior of this 124-room hotel.

➕ E4 ✉ Panská 12 ☎ 224 093 111; fax 224 221 240 🚇 Můstek

PAŘÍŽ

Rampant early 1900s splendour, with 93 rooms, in Staré město.

➕ E4 ✉ U Obecního domu 1 ☎ 222 195 195; fax 224 225 475; www.hotel-pariz.cz 🚇 Náměstí Republiky

PRAGUE HILTON ATRIUM

Around the vast interior atrium of the city's largest hotel are 788 rooms, enough to house Bill Clinton's entourage during his presidential visit to Prague in 1994.

➕ F3 ✉ Pobřežní 1 ☎ 224 841 111; fax 224 842 378 🚇 Florenc

PRAHA

The Praha perfectly expresses the way Communist taste moved from the Stalinist certainties of the International Hotel in the 1950s to the anonymous luxury of the 1970s. Until 1989, the 124-room Praha, in its hilltop location in the western suburb of Dejvice, was reserved for privileged and powerful Party people.

🚹 B2 ✉ Sušická 20, Dejvice ☎ 224 341 111; fax 224 311 218; www.htlpraha.cz 🚇 Dejvická 🚊 Tram 2, 20, 26 to Hadovka

RENAISSANCE

A comfortable, modern, 314-room hotel with all the facilities for business travellers. Tourists will appreciate its location a block from the Municipal House and the shops along Na příkopě. Operated by the Marriott organization.

🚹 F4 ✉ V Celnici 7, Nové Město ☎ 221 822 100; fax 221 822 200 🚇 Náměstí Republiky

SAVOY

Top-notch hotel near Prague Castle. This 61-room hotel has been completely modernized.

🚹 C4 ✉ Keplerova 6 ☎ 224 302 430; fax 224 302 128 🚊 Tram 22, 23 to Pohořelec

UNGELT

A nine-room apartment hotel in ancient premises that once formed part of the city's customs house, in Staré Město.

🚹 E4 ✉ Malá Štupartská 1 ☎ 224 828 686; fax 224 828 181 🚇 Náměstí Republiky

U PÁVA

The Peacock preens itself on its perfect location by the Vojan Gardens in lower Malá Strana, a few short steps from Charles Bridge. It has 11 rooms.

🚹 D4 ✉ U lužického semináře 32 ☎ 257 533 573; fax 257 530 484 🚇 Malostranská

U RAKA

Idyllically located among the stuccoed houses of Nový Svět. Extremely comfortable, rather exclusive.

🚹 C4 ✉ Černínská 10 ☎ 220 511 100; fax 233 358 041; www.romantik hotels. com/prag 🚊 Tram 22, 23 to Brusnice

U TŘÍ PŠTROSŮ

The Three Ostriches, in an exquisite gabled Renaissance building, was once the centre of a flourishing feather trade, later a coffee house. From some of the 18 rooms you can almost exchange a handshake with people passing by on Charles Bridge.

🚹 D4 ✉ Dražického náměstí 12 ☎ 257 532 410; fax 257 533 217 🚊 Tram 12, 22, 23 to Malostranské náměstí

VILLA VOYTA

The staff at this 20-room hotel in the southern suburbs cater to their mostly business clientele with great care, both in the original Secession villa and in the modern addition across the street.

🚹 Off map to south of the centre ✉ K novému dvoru 124/54, Lhotka ☎ 261 711 307; fax 244 471 248 🚇 Kačerov, then bus 106, 150, 170, 196, 203 to Sulická

ACCOMMODATION ADVICE

Any number of agencies at the airport, the main train station (Hlavní nádraží) and Holešovice train station stand ready to help you with accommodation advice. Two helpful agencies elsewhere are Accommodation Service (✉ Haštalská 7, Staré město, ☎ 231 0202), which offers apartments in the Old Town and further afield, and Stop City (✉ Vinohradská 24, Vinohrady ☎ 2252 1252), which rents a range of accommodation, mostly in the Vinohrady area.

A small apartment for two people in a good part of the city costs around Kč1,500–2,500 per night.

Prague Information Service (Pražská informační služba– PIS ☎ 221 714 130), the official city information agency, will also find lodgings. It has offices at the Old Town Hall and Na příkopě (➤ 20).

Mid-Range Hotels

PRICES

Expect to pay Kč2,500–5,000 for a double room in a mid-range hotel.

BREATHE FREELY

Choosing a place to stay requires care. A central location may turn out to be noisy with traffic as the rush hour gets under way shortly after 5am. Somewhere in the suburbs may seem a long way from the action, but if the hotel is near a Metro station this is unlikely to be a problem, and your night's rest may be more relaxed because you are breathing air that is fresher (albeit marginally so).

AMETYST

A fresh and inviting 84-room, family-owned hotel, the equal in luxury to most of the big names and only 10 minutes' walk from Wenceslas Square.

✚ F6 ✉ Jana Masaryka 11, Vinohrady ☎ 224 254 185; fax 224 251 315; www.hotel ametyst.cz 🚇 Náměstí Míru

ANNA

A reliable 23-room hotel in the pleasant inner suburb of Vinohrady, less than 15 minutes' stroll from Wenceslas Square.

✚ G5 ✉ Budečská 17, Vinohrady ☎ 222 513 111; fax 222 515 158 🚇 Náměstí Míru

APART-KAREE

Nine bright, clean apartments with small kitchens for one to five people. Free internet access.

✚ E5 ✉ Ve Smečkách 19, Nové Město ☎ 222 210 810; fax 222 210 809; www.karee.cz 🚇 Muzeum

BETLEM CLUB

A small 22-room hotel offering accommodation in the same square as Jan Hus's historic Bethlehem Chapel.

✚ E4 ✉ Betlémské náměstí 9 ☎ 222 221 574; fax 222 220 580; www.betlemclub.cz 🚇 Národní třída

CENTRAL

Somewhat sparce but quite adequate, the Central is located behind the Municipal House, with 68 rooms.

✚ E4 ✉ Rybná 8 ☎ 224 812 041 or 224 812 734; fax 222 328 404; www.cityhotels.cz 🚇 Náměstí Republiky

CLOISTER INN

Adequate 48-room hotel between the National Theatre and the Bethlehem Chapel.

✚ E4 ✉ Konviktská 14, Staré Město ☎ 224 211 020; fax 224 210 800 🚇 Národní třída

HAŠTAL

This simple 12-room hotel, situated in a former brewery, was reconstructed in 2003. Nice views over a quiet square.

✚ E4 ✉ Haštalská 16, Staré Město ☎ 222 314 335; www.hastal.com 🚋 Tram 5, 14, 26 to Dlouhá třída

HOTEL 16 U SV KATEŘINY

Excellent-value family hotel, with 14 rooms. Just around the corner from the Dvořák Museum and the botanical gardens, and 10 minutes' walk from Wenceslas Square.

✚ E5 ✉ Kateřinská 16 ☎ 224 920 636; fax 224 920 626; www.hotel16.cz 🚇 I P Pavlova

MAXIMILIAN

The historic 1904 building has been beautifully reconstructed in art-nouveau style with attention to every detail.

✚ E4 ✉ Haštalská 16, Staré Město ☎ 225 303 111; fax 225 303 119; www.maximilian hotel.com 🚋 Tram 5, 14, 26 to Dlouhá třída

NOVOMĚSTSKÝ HOTEL

A small hotel on a quiet street by the New Town Hall, with a high standard for the lowish room rates.

✚ E5 ✉ Řeznická 4, Nové Město ☎ 222 231 498; fax 222 233 052 🚇 Karlovo náměstí

OBORA

Well-appointed 21-room hotel in the royal hunting park and near Hvězda Castle, close to the airport.

🕂 Off map to west of the centre ✉ Libocká 271/1 ☎ 235 357 779; fax 235 366 093 🚇 Hradčanská, then tram 1, 18 to Petřiny

PÁV

A family-run, eight-room pension in a side street in Nové město where you'll also find Prague's most popular beer hall.

🕂 E5 ✉ Křemencova 13 ☎ 224 933 760; fax 224 933 080; www.pension-pav.cz 🚇 Národní třída

SAX

This 22-room hotel just off Nerudova Street offers superb views of Malá Strana.

🕂 C4 ✉ Janský vršek 3 ☎ 257 531 268; fax 257 534 101; www.sax.cz 🚋 Tram 12, 22, 23 to Malostranské náměstí then an uphill walk

SEIBER HOTEL & APARTMENTS

This gracious family-run establishment offers 20 luxurious rooms. A giant step up from the average mid-range hotel.

🕂 G5 ✉ Slezská 55, Vinohrady ☎ 224 250 025; fax 224 250 027; www.sieber.cz 🚇 Jiřího z Poděbrad 🚋 Tram 10, 16 to Perunova

TCHAIKOVSKY

A modest, tasteful 19-room hotel near Karlovo náměstí, the Dvořák museum and the botanical gardens.

🕂 E5 ✉ Ke Karlovu 19, Nové Město ☎ 224 912 121; fax 224 912 123; www.hoteltchaikovsky.com 🚋 Tram 4, 6, 10, 16, 22, 23 to Štěpánská

U KRÁLE JIŘÍHO

A small hotel just off the Royal Way with 11 comfortable rooms and the dubious bonus of a pub on the ground floor.

🕂 E4 ✉ Liliová 10, Staré Město ☎ 222 220 925; fax 222 221 707; www.kinggeorge.cz 🚇 Staroměstská

U LILIE

This 17-room pension is in a medieval house close to Charles Bridge.

🕂 E4 ✉ Liliová 15, Staré Město ☎ 222 220 432; fax 222 220 641; www.pensionulilie.cz 🚇 Staroměstská

U MEDVÍDKŮ

The 22-room pension features beautiful beamed ceilings. The famous pub of the same name is downstairs.

🕂 E4 ✉ Na Perštýne 7, Staré Město ☎ 224 211 916; fax 224 220 930; www.umedvidku.cz 🚇 Národní třída

U ŠUTERŮ

The large, bright rooms in this Gothic house are furnished with antiques.

🕂 E5 ✉ Palackého, Nové Město ☎ 224 948 235; fax 224 948 233; www.usuteru.cz 🚇 Národní třída

UNION

A 57-room art-nouveau hotel with comfortable and stylish rooms set in a quiet square.

🕂 E6 ✉ Ostrčilovo náměstí 4, Nusle ☎ 261 214 812; fax 261 214 820; www.hotelunion.cz 🚋 Tram 18, 24 to Ostrčilovo náměstí

SPECIAL OFFERS

The number of moderately priced hotels has increased rapidly, but these properties are probably still outnumbered by expensive hotels. However, it's always worth checking to see if the latter are offering any special deals, particularly for weekend stays.

BOTELS

An alternative to conventional hotels are the 'botels' moored at various points along the banks of the Vltava. However, being rather cramped, they are less romantic than they might sound. One such, close to the Palacký Bridge (Palackého most) on the Smíchov quayside, is the Admirál (☎ 257 321 302).

Budget Accommodation

PRICES

Expect to pay Kč1,000–2,500 for a double room in budget accommodation.

HOME AWAY FROM HOME

An economical solution to the problem of accommodation is to stay in a private house or, more likely, to rent an apartment. Most agencies have such places on their books, and going through one of them is better than allowing yourself to be solicited on arrival. Private rooms can also be booked from abroad. Check that you won't have to change buses and trams three times to get into town from your accommodation.

ATON

A friendly, family-run hotel with 16 clean, comfortable rooms. Close to the castle.
✚ A–B4 ✉ Na Petynce 37, Břevnov ☎ 233 350 376; fax 220 518 457 🚇 Hradčanská, then bus 108, 174 to Katjetánka

BERN

Reasonable comfort and facilities, rock-bottom prices at this simple hotel a brief bus ride east of the centre.
✚ G4 ✉ Kaněvova 29, Žižkov ☎ 222 584 420 🚇 Florenc, then bus 133, 207 to Tachovské

BÍLÝ LEV

A good-value, 27-room establishment in the eastern suburb of Žižkov.
✚ G4 ✉ Cimburkova 20 ☎ 222 780 430; fax 222 780 465 🚇 Trams 5, 9, 26 to Husinecká

CITY PENSION

Exceptionally pleasant 19-room pension, one Metro stop from Wenceslas Square.
✚ F6 ✉ Belgická 10, Vinohrady ☎ 222 521 606; fax 222 522 386; www.hotelcity.cz 🚇 Náměstí Míru

COUBERTIN

A modern 31-room hotel named after the founder of the modern Olympics and located among the Strahov sports facilities.
✚ B5 ✉ Atletická 4, Strahov ☎ 233 353 109; fax 220 513 208 🚇 Dejvická, then bus 149, 217 to Stadion Strahov

GOLF

This 163-room motel is handily located on the main road that heads into the city from the west.
✚ Off map to west of the centre. ✉ Plzeňská 215a, Motol ☎ 257 215 185; fax 257 215 213 🚇 Anděl, then tram 7, 9, 10, 58 to Hotel Golf

KAFKA

Good-value, 50-room hotel on the wrong side of the tracks in the inner suburb of Žižkov, but only 10 minutes' walk from the main train station and a short tram ride to Wenceslas Square.
✚ G4 ✉ Cimburkova 24 ☎ 222 781 333 🚇 Tram 5, 9, 26 to Husinecká

LOUDA

Pleasant eight-room pension on a residential road off the main highway to northern Bohemia and eastern Germany.
✚ H1 ✉ Kubišova 10, Troja ☎ 284 681 491; fax 284 681 488 🚇 Nádraží Holešovice, then tram 5, 14, 17 to Hercovka

MARKÉTA

Bright and cheery 26-room hotel in a quiet street close to the castle.
✚ A–B4 ✉ Na Petynce 45, Břevnov ☎ 220 518 316; fax 220 513 283; www.europehotels.cz 🚇 Hradčanská, then bus 108, 174 to Katjetánka

TŘÍSKA

A friendly place well sited in the pleasant Vinohrady neighbourhood. Each of the funkily-furnished rooms has a refrigerator. Cash only.
✚ G5 ✉ Vinohradská 105, Vinohrady ☎ 222 727 313; fax 222 723 562; www.hotel-triska.cz 🚇 Jiřího z Poděbrad

PRAGUE
travel facts

ESSENTIAL FACTS

Customs regulations

- The duty-free allowance is 200 cigarettes or 100 cigars or 250g tobacco; 2 litres of wine; 1 litre of spirits; and personal items totalling Kč6,000 in value.
- In principle, there are strict limits on the export of goods purchased in the Czech Republic, but normal tourist souvenirs are unlikely to pose a problem. Antiques and 'rare cultural objects' require an official certificate from a recognized museum or art gallery (which the dealer may already have obtained).

Electricity

- 230 volts, 50 cycles AC, fed through standard Continental two-pin plugs.

Etiquette

- Czech manners tend to be formal. Titles such as Doctor must not be ignored, and hands should be shaken when offered.
- Dress is less formal than it used to be. Neat casual wear is acceptable in most restaurants and tourist theatres. Smart dress is expected in other theatres and at the opera.
- Diners share tables in crowded restaurants and exchange greetings such as '*dobrý den*' ('good day') and '*dobrou chuť*' ('enjoy your meal').
- Czechs invariably say hello '*dobrý den*' and goodbye '*na shledanou*' when entering or leaving an establishment.
- If you are invited to a Czech home, take flowers or a gift and remove your shoes at the door.

Lavatories

- 'WC', '*muži/páni*' (Men), and '*ženy/dámy*' (Women) are useful signs to remember.

- Public facilities are rare; look in restaurants, cafés, etc.
- Tip the attendant with some smaller coins.

Money matters

- There are plenty of bureaux de change, but banks and ATMs often give better exchange rates.
- Credit cards are in increasing use, particularly in tourist spots.

National holidays

- 1 January, Easter Monday, 1 May (Labour Day), 8 May (Liberation Day), 5 July (SS Cyril and Methodius), 6 July (Jan Hus's Day), 28 September (St Wenceslas's Day), 28 October (Independence Day), 17 November (Day of Students), 24–26 December.

Opening hours

- Banks: Mon–Fri 8–5.
- Shops: many city-centre shops stay open until late weekdays and are also open weekends. In the suburbs and elsewhere, shops are open Mon–Fri 9–6; Sat 9–1.
- Museums and galleries: Tue–Sun 9/10–5. Most close Mon, except the National Museum and Prague Castle (open daily); the Jewish Museum is open Sun–Fri. Some museums also close for lunch.

Places of worship

- Roman Catholic: sv Tomáše (St Thomas's Church) ✉ Josefská 8, Malá Strana 🚇 Malostranská 🕐 English mass Sun 11am
- Anglican: sv Klimenta (St Clement's Church) ✉ Klimentská, Nové Město 🚇 Náměstí Republiky 🕐 English-language service Sun 11am
- Jewish: Staronová synagóga (Old/New Synagogue, ➤ 39) ✉ Pařížská and Červená 🚇 Staroměstská

🕐 Services Mon–Thu 8am; Fri sundown; Sat 9am
- Interdenominational:
  International Church of Prague
  ✉ Peroutkova 57, Smíchov 🚇 Anděl
  🕐 Service Sun 10.30am

Student travellers
- Few discounts are available for students, but keeping out of the most popular tourist spots makes Prague an affordable city.
- All aspects of youth travel are dealt with by the Student Agency
  ✉ Ječná 377, Nové Město ☎ 224 999 666
  🚇 I P Pavlova

Women travellers
- Women travellers need take no more than the usual precautions.
- At night, unaccompanied females lingering around Wenceslas Square may be taken for prostitutes.

GETTING AROUND

- Public transport maps are available from the Prague Information Service (► 20) and from the information centres at Metro stations Muzeum, Můstek, Anděl, Černý Most and Nádraží Holešovice.
- Expect crowding during the rush hours (generally 7am–10am, 3pm–6pm). The young and fit should give up their seats to passengers who need them more.

Metro
- This showpiece system, with its fast and frequent trains and clean stations, consists of three lines: A (colour-coded green), B (yellow) and C (red). They converge from the suburbs onto the city centre where there are several interchange stations.
- To get on the right train, check the line (A, B or C) and note the name of the terminus station at

the end of the line in the direction you wish to travel; this station appears on the overhead direction signs.
- Outlying stations are relatively far apart and are intended to feed commuters to connecting trams and buses.
- Particularly useful stations are Můstek (for Wenceslas Square and Old Town Square), Staroměstská (for Old Town Square) and Malostranská (for Malá Strana and for trams 22 and 23). Hradčanská station is 15 minutes' walk from Prague Castle.

Tram
- The tramway system operates in close conjunction with the Metro.
- The name of every tram stop appears on the stop sign and on the route map.
- Tram routes are numbered, and the tram has a destination board. Timetables are pasted on the stop and are almost always adhered to.
- There is a skeleton service of night trams, with its own system of numbers and schedules.
- A particularly useful and scenic line is the No. 22/23, which runs from the city centre (at Národní třída) right through Malá Strana, past Malostranská Metro station, then climbs to the back of Prague Castle (Pražský hrad stop) and continues to Strahov Monastery.

Bus
- Kept out of the city centre to minimise pollution, buses serve all the suburban areas that the trams do not reach.

Discounts
- Special passes are available but are useful only if you intend to make lots of trips.

Taxi

- Prague taxi drivers have a reputation for overcharging.
- Agree on the approximate fare beforehand. Ask for a receipt to reduce excessive demands.
- You may receive a more reliable service if you phone for a taxi or flag down a moving taxi rather than going to a taxi rank in a tourist area, where drivers have the worst reputation.
- For taxis, telephone AAA Radiotaxi ☎ 14014 or Profitaxi ☎ 14035
- Upmarket hotels have their own taxi service, reliable but expensive.

COMMUNICATIONS

Telephones

- Ongoing modernization of the Czech phone system means improved service. In September 2002, the entire system was digitalized and everyone received a new, 9-digit number. With the exception of emergency numbers, taxi dispatchers and the like, anything but a 9-digit number is no longer valid. If in doubt, call directory inquiries ☎ 1180.
- Most public phones now take phone cards, on sale in kiosks and post offices.
- Telephoning from your hotel may cost four times the standard rate.
- To call the Czech Republic from the UK, dial 00 420. To call the UK from Prague, dial 00 44, then drop the first zero from the area code.
- To call the Czech Republic from the US, dial 00420. To call the US from Prague, dial 001

Mail

- Postage stamps can be bought at post offices, kiosks and hotels.

- The main post office, with fax and poste restante services, is at ✚ F4 ✉ Jindřišská 14, Nové Město ☎ 221 131 445 🚇 Můstek.

EMERGENCIES

Sensible precautions

- Despite some horror stories, Prague is still safer than most comparable Western cities.
- The main hazard is pickpockets in the tourist areas – Charles Bridge, Wenceslas Square and Old Town Square. Hold onto your handbag and don't carry your wallet or passport in your back pocket.
- A common scam is for someone to accost you with an innocent-seeming enquiry about money or the location of the nearest bank. His 'policeman' accomplice will then appear and relieve you of your passport if you are unwise enough to produce it.

Lost property

- The lost property office is at ✉ Karoliny Světlé 5, Staré Město ☎ 224 235 085

Medical treatment

- UK citizens are entitled to free emergency medical treatment. However, it is advisable for visitors to take out medical insurance.
- Foreigners' Polyclinic ✉ Roentgenova 2, Motol (off map) ☎ 257 272 146; 257 271 111 (nights and weekends) 🚍 Bus 167 from Anděl Metro to the last stop Bring your passport to this former Communist Party clinic, which is part of the Nemocnice Na Homolce, the huge hospital complex just off the main highway to Pilsen in the western suburb of Motol. It is the best place to go for serious treatment.
- Fakultní poliklinika (✚ E5 ✉ Karlovo náměstí 32, Nové Město ☎ 224 904

111 🌐 Mon–Fri 7–3.30 🚇 Karlovo náměstí) is a city-centre alternative to the above for less serious ailments.

- Drugs prescribed locally must be paid for.
- Remember to bring supplies of any regular medication you take with you.
- 24-hour pharmacies (*lékárna*) are at ✉ Palackého 5, Nové Město and ✉ Belgická 37, Vinohrady

Emergency phone numbers
- Ambulance ☎ 155
- Police ☎ 158
- Fire brigade ☎ 150

Embassy
- UK ➕ D4 ✉ Thunovská 14, Malá Strana ☎ 257 402 111 🚇 Malostranská, then tram 12, 22, 23
- US ➕ D4 ✉ Tržiště 15, Malá Stana ☎ 257 530 663 🚋 Tram 12, 22, 23 to Malostranská

LANGUAGE

- Czech is a Slavic language, so anyone who knows other Slavic languages, such as Russian or Polish, should muddle through.
- It will be rewarding to master a few words and phrases, if only to be able to ask if anyone speaks your language and to recognize some signs.
- Czech is pronounced as it is written (unlike English).

Vowels
a as in mammoth   á as in father
e as in yes   é as in air
i,y as in city   í,ý as in meet
o as in top   ó as in more
u as in book   ú,ů as in boom

Consonants
c as in its   č as in china
ch as in Scottish loch
j as in yes   ň as in onion

r rolled or trilled r ř combination of r and z (as in Dvořák)
š as in shine
z as in zero
ž as in pleasure

Basic words and phrases
yes ano no ne
please prosím thank you děkuji
do you speak English/German? mluvíte anglicky /německy?
I don't understand nerozumím
I don't speak Czech nemluvím česky
hello (informal) ahoj
good morning/good day dobrý den
good evening dobrý večer
goodbye na shledanou
sorry promiňte
where? kde? how much? kolik?
when? kdy? what co?

Numbers
1	jeden/jedna/	11	jedenáct
2	dva/dvě	12	dvanáct
3	tři	13	třináct
4	čtyři	14	čtrnáct
5	pět	15	patnáct
6	šest	16	šestnáct
7	sedm	17	sedmnáct
8	osm	18	osmnáct
9	devět	19	devatenáct
10	deset	20	dvacet

Days of the week
Monday pondělí Friday pátek
Tuesday úterý Saturday sobota
Wednesday středa Sunday neděle
Thursday čtvrtek

Useful words
beer pivo big velký/á/é
bus or tram stop zastávka
café kavárna castle hrad
closed zavřeno open otevřeno
entrance vchod/vstup
exit východ/výstup
Danger! pozor! forbidden zákaz
station nádraží water voda

Index

CityPack
Prague *Top 25*

ABOUT THE AUTHOR

Michael Ivory's passion for Prague is a long-standing one. He is both a landscape architect and freelance travel writer, and lectures on the city and revisits it whenever possible. His books for the AA include *Essential Hungary*, *Essential Czech Republic* and *Explorer Prague*.

WRITTEN BY   Michael Ivory
EDITION REVISER AND CONTRIBUTIONS TO "LIVING PRAGUE" Jenny Becker
MANAGING EDITORS   Apostrophe S Limited
COVER DESIGN   Tigist Getachew, Fabrizio La Rocca

A CIP catalogue record for this book is available from the British Library.

ISBN 0 7495 4017 6
ISBN 978 0 7495 4017 3

Published by AA Publishing, a trading name of Automobile Association Developments Limited, whose registered office is Southwood East, Apollo Rise, Farnborough, Hampshire, GU14 0JW. Registered number 1878835.

© **AUTOMOBILE ASSOCIATION DEVELOPMENTS LIMITED 1996, 1999, 2002, 2004**
First published 1996. Revised second edition 1999. Reprinted Oct 1999, Apr, Dec 2000. Revised third edition 2002. Reprinted May 2002. Revised fourth edition 2004. Reprinted 2004 (three times)

Colour separation by Daylight Colour Art Pte Ltd., Singapore
Printed and bound by Hang Tai D&P Limited, Hong Kong

ACKNOWLEDGEMENTS

The Automobile Association would like to thank the following agencies and libraries for their assistance in the preparation of this title.
AKG London 29; Embassy of the Czech Republic, London; 17r, Michael Ivory, 27t, 27b; National Gallery in Prague 49; Stockbyte 5

The remaining images are held in the Association's own library (AA WORLD TRAVEL LIBRARY) and were taken by Jon Wyand, with the exception of 8cl, 10cr, 11crt, 13cl, 13cr, 14c, 18cl, 22b, 24c, 24cr which were taken by Simon McBride; 7tl, 7tc, 8bl, 8cb, 8/9, 9r, 10cl, 11crb, 12cl, 16t, 16l, 16r, 20cr, 20c, 28c, 30t, 31, 32t, 34b, 38b, 39, 40b, 50t, 51b, 52, 54, 56, 57, 58, 60, 63b, 89b which were taken by Clive Sawyer and 9t, 10t, 12t, 12cr, 13t, 14t, 16t, 18t, 20tl, 22tl, 23, 24t, 24cl, 25b, 26, 35, 38t, 43t, 44t, 48t, 48b, 89t which were taken by Anthony Souter

A02432
Maps © Automobile Association Developments Limited 1996, 1999, 2002
Fold out map © Mairs Geographischer Verlag / Falk Verlag, 73751 Ostfildern
Transport map © TCS, Aldershot, England